Swarthm

GW00384538

ONLY FELLOW-VOYAGERS

creation stories as guides for the journey

Anne Thomas

Quaker Home Service & Woodbrooke College
for the
Swarthmore Lecture Committee

First published May 1995
by Quaker Home Service
& Woodbrooke College
for the
Swarthmore Lecture Committee

ISBN 0 85425 272 1

Cover by John Blamires

PREFACE

The Swarthmore Lectureship was established by the Woodbrooke Extension Committee at a meeting held on the 9th December 1907: the minute of the Committee provided for an 'annual lecture on some subject relating to the message and work of the Society of Friends'. The name 'Swarthmore' was chosen in memory of the home of George and Margaret Fox, which was always open to the earnest seeker after Truth, and from which loving words of sympathy and substantial material help were sent to fellow workers.

The lectureship has a twofold purpose: first, to interpret to the members of the Religious Society of Friends their message and mission; secondly, to bring before the public the spirit, the aims and fundamental principles of Friends. The lecturers alone are responsible for any opinions expressed.

The lectureship provides both for the publication of a book and for the delivery of a lecture, the latter usually at the time of assembly of the Yearly Meeting of the Religious Society of Friends (Quakers) in Britain. A lecture related to the present book was delivered at Friends House, Euston Road, London, on the evening of the 6th May 1995.

It is a century now since Darwin gave us the first glimpse of the origin of species. We know now what was unknown to all the preceding caravan of generations: that men are *only fellow-voyagers** with other creatures in the odyssey of evolution. This new knowledge should have given us, by this time, a sense of kinship with fellow-creatures; a wish to live and let live, a sense of wonder over the magnitude and duration of the biotic enterprise.

Above all, we should, in the century since Darwin, have come to know that man, while now captain of the adventuring ship, is hardly the sole object of its quest, and that his prior assumptions to this effect arose from the simple necessity of whistling in the dark.

Aldo Leopold, *A Sand County Almanac*,
Oxford University Press, 1949,
Ballantine edition 1970,
pages 116-117

* lecturer's italics

CONTENTS

ACKNOWLEDGEMENTS

Without the support of my 'minders', David Gray and Janet Scott, the invitation from the Swarthmore Lecture Committee might not have been accepted. Throughout the gestation period, David and Janet kept in touch, even sharing lunch with me in British Columbia! David's clear and kindly critique has tightened the text and removed any Canadianisms that might have slipped in, eh?

Jim Pym and David Goddard worked with diligence on the technical aspects of production. I am grateful to Geoffrey Makins who drafted the diagram on page 32 and to John Blamires who designed the cover.

The Spirit of Haida Gwaii has been my constant companion. The Museum of Civilization in Hull, Quebec, has the white plaster pattern on display, but it does not have the power of the black bronze canoe which heads resolutely for the Capitol building in Washington, D.C.

Other special companions are my fellow General Secretaries from Baltimore, New England, New York, and Philadelphia Yearly Meetings and the Field Secretaries with whom I have gathered in retreat most Springs for the last several years. Thank you for your understanding and unfailing support. Johan Maurer, General Secretary of Friends United Meeting, has been my prayer partner for two years and his faith spans the distance between Ottawa, Ontario and Richmond, Indiana.

My life would be simpler, more restful, but much less rewarding, without the members and attenders of Canadian Yearly Meeting. It has been a privilege to work for Friends and to represent them on various ecumenical bodies, where

I found further soul-mates and fellow-voyagers. Bill Gilbert has been a long-time travelling companion on the back roads of eastern Ontario.

Finally, I wish to thank my family for the love they bring to my life. Barry, Helen and Simon will each have different reasons for disagreeing with parts of this text, but their support and challenge provide me with a deep source of inspiration and joy. My late father, Jack Walker, always offered me unconditional love which continues to ground me during stormy times.

Chapter I

THE SPIRIT OF HAIDA GWAII

IN the Canadian Chancery in Washington, D.C. stands a large sculpture named *The Spirit of Haida Gwaii*[1], that is The Spirit of the Islands of the People. This is a canoe filled with characters from the myths of the Haida Nation of the Queen Charlotte Islands, which are off the northwest coast of British Columbia. These characters do not all appear in any one traditional story, but the artist, Bill Reid, visualised them journeying together.

At the stern we see the Raven, a trickster, holding the steering oar. Under his tail is the Mouse Woman, guide and adviser to those human beings who undertake journeys into the spirit world. In the bow is the Grizzly Bear, and near him sits his human wife, the Bear Mother. Between them are their children, the Two Cubs. Bill Reid gives these cubs non-traditional names, Bad Bear and Good Bear, which are taken from a poem by A. A. Milne. The Beaver, one of the Raven's uncles, sits behind the Bear Mother, and behind the Beaver is the Dogfish Woman who is part human and part shark. The Eagle sits above the Frog. The Wolf stretches across the centre of the canoe with his claws in the Beaver's back and his teeth in the Eagle's wing. The chief Kilstlaai stands in the centre of the melée. Kilstlaai's robe and staff incorporate further characters, the Seabear and the Killer Whale. A new addition to the characters of the myths is a human paddler, a self-portrait of the sculptor, whom Reid has named the Ancient Reluctant Conscript. Both human beings and animals are crowded into this dugout canoe.

As they paddle together, heading for an unknown destination, each is uncomfortable in the others' presence.

Bill Reid discovered his Haida heritage as an adult and many others have been able to get in touch with the power of Haida stories through his art. Reid feels free to reinterpret these old and traditional stories in ways which speak to his present condition.

Many Canadians who view *The Spirit of Haida Gwaii* see references in it to the national political scene. Tensions between Ontario and the western provinces, the desire of many Quebecers to separate from Canada, and the land claims of our First Nations, are all present in the complexity of myth, political and sexual symbolism given form by the sculpture.

When I first saw photographs of this work, Noah's ark came to mind, occupied not only by Noah, his family and the animals, but also by Adam and Eve, the snake, Cain and Abel, and the other descendants of Adam and Eve, right down to the builders of Babel, that is, all the characters of the early chapters of Genesis.

What would happen on such a voyage? Would humankind need to look again at our relationship to each other and to all of creation? Who would survive? Can we re-vision the stories which have been formative for earlier generations, and discern from them a meaning for our lives and times?

The stories of Genesis 1-11 tell of origins and relationships. For many generations of hearers and readers they gave a sense of place, personal identity, gender identity, relationship to God, to each other and creation, and the purpose of existence. They shaped a series of societies' views of their past, present and future.

Today the word 'story' has lost its power. It is often used as a synonym for 'untruth', as in, 'Don't tell stories, dear.'

There is also an ambivalence in the understanding of the word 'myth'. It is used by scholars to describe a story which has superhuman beings as its characters, is set in otherworldly time and space, and which reveals some cosmic dimensions of the culture. In everyday use 'myth', like 'story', contains the element of 'fairy story', and the power recognised by earlier hearers has been lost. We tend to assume that these stories no longer transmit values, yet our language and speech are still infused with mythological terms. Though many people have not read for themselves the Old Testament, the Greek myths or Shakespeare, the characters of these stories are part of our culture, being known by name and by particular characteristics. These characteristics may not be the ones intended by the original author and may have been added by later interpreters.

As sophisticated individuals, living at the end of the twentieth century, we may assume that our values are acquired through careful, detached and unbiased thought, but in reality most human beings negotiate values through story, rather than through legal argument or philosophical debate. This is very evident among members of the First Nations in Canada. With the coming of the 'two founding nations' of French and English settlers, the culture of Europe was imposed on these peoples. The sad history of decline over the past three hundred years is often represented by pictures of inebriated men and women sitting on a city curb, or of grubby children sniffing glue on a reserve. With the re-owning of their stories and ceremonies, First Nations' peoples are regaining meaning and purpose in their lives.

We tend to consign the stories in Genesis 1-11 to First Day (Sunday) School classes, and in doing so, simplify them to such an extent that both their positive messages and challenging problems are smoothed away. Having done our duty, we then close the book and are unlikely to return to these stories.

What narratives shape us today? We seem to have rejected the traditional ones. Perhaps the search for meaning, often described as New Age spirituality, reflects the vacuum people are experiencing. Any narrative that shapes us is shared, enacted and tested before it is embedded in our culture and in our individual lives. The content of the narrative is truthful if it remains open to challenge and change. A narrative that can accept new interpretations and still have power may lead a community to new life.[2]

Theology is 'God talk'. If we open the Bible at page one, the first theologians we encounter are the serpent and the woman in Genesis 3:1-5. They speak about God in terms of their particular interests and needs. Janet Scott indicates that theology should be contemporary and inclusive. Contemporary in that it speaks to and of the world we know, reflects the way we think and deals with current problems. Inclusive in that it involves the whole personality, is moral towards people and God, and is aware of and avoids dismissively judging others.[3]

The Bible is a record of how succeeding generations discussed and interpreted earlier theologies and discerned a contemporary meaning for their times. In reaching these meanings, they were influenced by their own experiences, other Near Eastern religious traditions and re-interpretations of the biblical tradition itself. As early Friends sought to regain the spirit of the early Church they used the Bible as a written source as they experienced love and unity with God and each other.[4] As we look at the experience of the biblical authors and of early Friends, we need to see how the environment in which they lived affected their God-talk. We may then be better able to identify the signs of our times, out of which we may discern a theology which relates to our experience.

A quotation from Isaiah may be used as an example of this chain of experience and re-interpretation of a particular text. About six hundred years before the birth of Jesus, the prophet Isaiah offered encouragement and hope to his people who were in exile in Babylon. He called them to believe that God would liberate them to become a nation which lived up to high ideals:

> The spirit of the Lord GOD is upon me,
> because the LORD has anointed me;
> he has sent me to bring good news to the oppressed,
> to bind up the brokenhearted,
> to proclaim liberty to the captives,
> and release to the prisoners;
> to proclaim the year of the LORD's favour.
>
> *Isaiah 61:1-2a*

When Jesus read this text in the synagogue at Nazareth, he used it as the basis of his own ministry and to challenge his hearers to take up the old prophetic call. He further re-interpreted the text by linking it to Elijah and Elisha's ministries to individuals who were often excluded from the community,[5] challenging his congregation to extend this good news, as Elijah and Elisha did, to gentile women and lepers.[6]

When George Fox quoted Isaiah 61:1, he challenged the Jews to recognise Jesus as the fulfilment of biblical prophecy.[7] For Margaret Fell, the quotations from Isaiah and Luke became a platform for her to address 'professed teachers', who quoted Luke 4 as their authority, rather than bringing the Spirit of Truth directly to their congregations.[8]

Canadian Yearly Meeting, seeking unity on prison abolition in 1981, experienced the liberating power of this text as they met in worship: '... We are increasingly clear that the imprisonment of human beings, like their enslavement, is inherently immoral and is as destructive to the cagers as to the caged ...'[9] Our own experience was the starting point for interpreting the text and included personal experiences, and experience of society, the world and the Divine.

Not all biblical verses or their traditional interpretations may be helpful to us in viewing our experience in a meaningful way; but we need to approach them with study, prayer and worshipful sharing to see if there is a new interpretation which speaks to our need,[10] before we reject them as having no place in our lives.

We have rejected the value of the biblical witness too easily, especially that of the Old Testament, and do not have available other resources with which to replace them.

'In the beginning ...' Most of us recognise these as the opening words of the book of Genesis, even if we rarely read the Bible. We also know of a second creation story which involves Adam, Eve and the snake, and many of us feel these, along with much of the biblical record, have little to say to our condition today.

For those of us with scientific training, our education may have incorporated a view of the Bible as pre-scientific. Science has been held up as the answer to all things, but many people are recognising that science alone cannot be the sole source of values. Scientific theories cannot embody and embrace deep meaning for our lives, and scientists are increasingly recognising this. For others, the Bible's attitude towards violence, slaves, women or homosexuals may have relegated it to a bottom shelf. Having rejected traditional stories and myths which can be the source of a set of values, we may ironically describe our current state by a short story: a society which had a variety of complete moral systems was subjected to a flood (a moral deluge?) leaving only a few islands visible in a sea of chaos. As there was no mainland, debate was useless, for there were no connecting principles on which to build.[11] Almost thirty years ago, historian Lynn White, Jr. shook both scientific and theological communities with his article *The Historical Roots of our Ecologic Crisis*,[12] in which he named the Judeo-Christian dogma of creation as the root cause of the destruction of the planet.

The stories in Genesis 1-11 have been given many different interpretations since their composition. Some had a long oral history before they were written down. The final editor of the book of Genesis took earlier writings and brought them together to fill the need of the community at the time of editing.[13] The early church inherited the text and added its own christological overlay, and the last two millennia have added many more layers of meaning. Is there anything these stories can say to us today? Are we prepared to give them a close reading before we relegate them to history?

Readers may find that the following chapters need a companion volume, The Bible. The translation I am using is the *New Revised Standard Version*. This version is shaped by the restrictions of the English language, and especially in chapters 2 and 3 of Genesis these cause problems when the word 'man' is used in several ways, a reflection also of the influence of culture.

In this book I will give chapters one through eleven of Genesis a close reading in an attempt to identify the intent of the original writers. Who was their intended audience? What was the background out of which they wrote? Did they have a particular bias? Secondly, I will examine how later biblical writers used the texts for their purposes. The Christian church also added layers of interpretation to the biblical text, but few of these will be considered in detail. Instead I will move directly to the use that early Friends made of Genesis 1-11, as they sought to experience the Spirit which inspired the original writers. To conclude, the topics covered by the Genesis stories will be examined. Do these stories contain themes which are relevant to our present and future?

The horizon we bring to these stories is that of educated men and women living at the end of the twentieth century, in a culture strongly shaped by the Christian re-visioning of the Hebrew scriptures, the scientific revolution and its subsequent developments. The stories we are looking at were written in the Near East 2,500 to 3,000 years ago, by men,[14] in constant struggle to live in a land they believed their god had given them.

We also come as Friends. Our Quaker tradition recognises the Bible as a primary written source of spiritual insight when read in openness to the inspiration of the Holy Spirit, but the Bible takes a secondary role to the direct experience of the living Christ.[15] George Fox did not consider the scriptures to be the Word of God, for he experienced Jesus Christ as the Word: 'The scriptures of truth are the words of God and not the word; and Christ who was before the scriptures were given forth, by whom the world was made, is the word of God, who fulfilled the words.'[16] The introduction to *Advices and Queries* states,

> Friends maintain that expressions of faith must be related to personal experience. Some find traditional Christian language full of meaning; some do not. Our understanding of our own religious tradition may sometimes be enhanced by insights of other faiths. The deeper realities of our faith are beyond precise verbal formulation and our way of worship based on silent waiting testifies to this.[17]

Even the naming of God is problematic for some Friends, who find the word patriarchal and linked to the distortions of some aspects of Christianity.[180] We may need to ask whether it is our resources of language which are obsolete rather than to ask whether God is dead.[19]

However, I do need to use language to communicate with you, and at this stage of my journey I choose to use the word 'God' but to avoid the regular use of 'He' or 'His'. I use 'humankind' when speaking of both men and women, and have chosen not to change the words of others in direct quotations, recognising that the words reflect their culture and experience. I bring to this text my life experience which has been shaped by many factors. I am a woman, from a working class family in the north of England. Excellent education and health care were made accessible to my generation by the *1944 Education Act* and the *1948 Health Act*. The excitement of Liverpool in The Beatles' era was part of my student life. I trained as a science teacher, taught in middle and grammar schools in Yorkshire and Merseyside, and married a toxicologist. After emigrating to Canada, and being accepted into membership of the Society of Friends by Ottawa Monthly Meeting, I was brought up by my children, as I balanced home-making with studies in religion and later the teaching of religion. My home is in a small village and we enjoy water from our own well. I presently work for Friends and find deep enrichment in ecumenical contacts. My spiritual life has periods of deep connections with all creation, and other desert times. I express my spiritual experiences using Christian metaphors tempered by the holistic view of Taoism. Some Friends accept me as a Christian, others do not. Each of these factors affects the way I approach the text of Genesis 1-11.

✳   ✳   ✳

As we face major crises in our life on the Earth, we do not expect God to pick one family, like that of Noah, to repopulate the Earth after a devastating flood. But like people of all eras, we do need a faith context out of which we can take ownership of challenges such as that expressed by Fred Hoyle in 1948: 'Once a photograph of Earth, taken from the outside, is available, an idea as powerful as any in history will be let loose.'[20] We now have that photograph:

> In the middle of the twentieth century, we saw our planet from space for the first time. Historians may eventually find that this vision has a greater impact on thought than did the Copernican revolution of the six-teenth century.[21a]

> It is so small and so fragile, and such a precious little spot in the universe, that you can block it out with your thumb, and you realise that on this small spot, that little blue and white thing, is everything that means anything to you - all of history, and music and poetry and art and war and death and birth, and love, tears, joy, games, all of it is on that little spot out there that you can cover with your thumb.[21b]

> Viewed from the distance of the moon, the aston-ishing thing about the earth, catching the breath, is that the earth is alive... the only exuberant thing in this part of the cosmos. If you could look long enough, you would see the swirling of the great drifts of white cloud, cover-ing and uncovering the half-hidden masses of land. If you had been looking for a very long, geological time, you could have seen the continents themselves in mo-tion, drifting apart on their crustal plates, held afloat by the fire beneath. It has the organized, self-contained look of a live creature, full of information, marvellously skilled in handling the sun.[22]

We must take the risk of entering the canoe with all our personal baggage and with those conscripts with whom we may be less than comfortable,[23] if we are to seek out and share, adapt and own the stories which will be our guide as we journey together.

✳   ✳   ✳

Do you welcome the diversity of culture, language and expressions of faith in our yearly meeting and in the world community of Friends? Seek to increase your understanding and to gain from this rich heritage and wide range of spiritual insights. Uphold your own and other yearly meetings in your prayers.

Do you respect that of God in everyone though it may be expressed in unfamiliar ways or be difficult to discern? Each of us has a particular experience of God and each must find the way to be true to it. When words are strange or disturbing to you, try to sense where they come from and what has nourished the lives of others. Listen patiently and seek the truth which other people's opinions may contain for you. Avoid hurtful criticism and provocative language. Do not allow the strength of your convictions to betray you into making statements or allegations that are unfair or untrue. Think it possible you may be mistaken.[24]

Chapter II

IN THE BEGINNING:
GENESIS 1:1-2:4A

GENESIS 1:1-2:4a, the first account of creation, is orderly and majestic, and raises only a few problems for us on a first reading, but critical readers may find it fraught with challenges, especially when they reach verse 26 with its 'have dominion over'. Genesis 1 is among the latest parts of the Hebrew scriptures[1] to be written. It took shape long after the Exodus experience (1450-1275 BCE[2]), the founding of the Davidic monarchy (1010 BCE) and the witness of the early prophets (850 BCE onwards). The chapter was probably written between 550 and 450 BCE in response to the experience of the Exile in Babylon (597-538 BCE). During this time of exile, the priestly leadership maintained and rebuilt the dispersed communities by the codification of law and the development of a literature which uniquely defined and separated the Jews[3] from the surrounding nations.

Before the Exile, the Israelites had struggled to gain and maintain possession of land they believed to be 'the Promised Land'. This land was occupied by the Canaanites whose religion was based on the worship of nature gods. El was the kind and benign creator who lived at the source of the rivers. Baal was the most prominent god, with power over storms and fertility. His consort was Anat, also known as Asherah or Ashtoreth. There were lesser, local gods and goddesses. Human sacrifice and sacred prostitution were common. In spite of its condemnation of this religion, the Bible includes many echoes of Canaanite faith and practice.[4]

The most pervasive influence may have been that of the Sumerians. Sumer was one of the major cultural centres of the Near East, and its cuneiform writing was borrowed by other cultures. Most Sumerian documents were composed by 2000 BCE, including stories of creation, fall, flood and the quest for immortality.[5]

There is no direct evidence that the Israelites had their own cosmological myths, though clues to the existence of a cosmology, based on those of the surrounding cultures, are sprinkled throughout the Hebrew scriptures. These can be collected into a narrative account:

Yahweh with one word created the Sun, the Moon, and the Stars. He stretched out the skies like a tent cloth over the Deep, and placed his secret court above the skies, founding it upon the Higher Waters. In creating, Yahweh rode above the Deep, which rose against Him. Tehom, queen of the Deep, sought to drown out Yahweh's Creation, but He rode against her in his chariot of fire, and bombarded her with hail and with lightening. Yahweh destroyed her vassal Leviathan with one great blow to his monster's skull, while he ended Rahab by thrusting a sword into his heart. The waters fled backward, awed by the voice of Yahweh, and Tehom fearfully surrendered. Yahweh shouted his triumph, and dried up the floods. He set the Moon to divide the seasons, the Sun to divide day and night. Observing Yahweh's victory, the Morning Stars sang together, and all the sons of God shouted for joy. Thus the work of Creation was completed.[6]

Instead of grounding their faith in a mythical cosmology like the other nations, the community looked to a particular historical event which shaped them as a nation. This was the exodus from Egypt.

The Exodus story, rather than the account of creation, is the foundation of Jewish faith, reflecting the consciousness of a people who know that they have been freed by their god from oppression. The concept of covenant undergirds and formalizes this relationship. Covenant is therefore built into the stories which were written later, and which sought to explain the nation's origins, based on their experience and relationship with a liberating god.

In Babylon, the exiles found themselves in a culture which was based on the creation myth entitled the *Enuma Elish*.[7] This was a reworking of earlier stories to celebrate the power of Babylon and its god Marduk over other cities and gods. The myth describes 'not only a new social order, but a new psychology'.[8]

The earliest religious symbols which have been found date back to 22,000 BCE and are representations of mother goddesses.[9] From the introduction of Babylonian mythology onwards, around 2000 BCE, the goddess became associated with nature as a chaotic force to be mastered as the newly dominant god took on the task of conquest. This polarization led to a patriarchal system which incorporated a series of dualisms: father god and mother goddess, a struggle between the two, the god represented good and was associated with light while the goddess represented nature or evil and was associated with darkness.

In the beginning, according to the *Enuma Elish,* were two oceans, the male Apsu and the female Tiamat, from which issued the younger gods. The noise of these younger gods irritated Apsu who plotted to kill them, but the plot was discovered and it was Apsu who was killed. Tiamat pledged revenge but she was murdered by Marduk. This cosmic battle was engraved on seven tablets. Tiamat's corpse became the cosmos. When the gods realised that they needed servants, Marduk was killed and his blood was mixed with clay to make human beings.

This Monty Pythonesque scenario was re-enacted by the Babylonians during their new year celebrations from 1700 BCE onwards for a period of more than 1,000 years. These were held in spring, after the emergence of dry land from the winter floods of the Tigris and Euphrates rivers. The king took the role of Marduk, during which time he was humiliated, revived and liberated. The enactment ended with a sacred marriage to revive the life-giving forces in nature and humanity. This ceremony ensured that chaos would be subdued for another year. Ziggurats, which were representations of celestial palaces, maintained the link between earth and the gods during the rest of the year.

The Babylonians believed that creation occurred through an act of violence where order (Marduk) was established over chaos (Tiamat). Human beings were the product of deicide, and women were identified with anarchy. The king constantly imposed order on his subjects who were slaves to the cult. Leisure was a privilege of the aristocracy who saw themselves as earthly representatives of the gods.

To a people in exile, the violent Babylonian gods may have seemed to have conquered the god of Israel who had liberated them from slavery in Egypt. Isaiah encouraged the exiles to remember that:

> There is no other god besides me,
> a righteous God and a Saviour;
> There is no one besides me.

> *Isaiah 45:21*

and exhorted Yahweh[10] to reveal his power over the creatures of Babylonian and Canaanite myth, while evoking the memory of crossing of the Red Sea:

> Awake, awake, put on strength, O arm of the LORD!
> Awake, as in days of old, the generations of long ago!

Was it not you who cut Rahab in pieces, who pierced
the dragon?
Was it not you who dried up the sea, the waters of the
great deep;
who made the depths of the sea a way for the
redeemed to cross over?
So the ransomed of the LORD shall return and come to
Zion with singing;

Isaiah 51:9-11

Isaiah experienced God as transcendent and beyond human comprehension, very different from the larger-than-life
human characteristics of the local pantheon:

For My thoughts are not your thoughts,
Nor are My ways your ways, says the LORD.
For as the heavens are higher than the earth,
so are My ways higher than your ways,
and My thoughts than your thoughts.

Isaiah 55:8-9

The epic genre of most Near Eastern literature was affected
by the *Enuma Elish*, whose influence can be traced through
Hittite, Assyrian, Persian, Canaanite, Hebrew, Greek and
Roman mythologies. Sympathetic magic was part of the
belief system; if humankind mimicked the behaviour of the
gods, the same scenario would be repeated on earth.

In contrast, the Bible focuses on the actions of God in
history, in real time, in the lives of real people. In Genesis 1
the priestly writers created a remarkably unmythical
liturgical statement which appropriated materials from
Babylonian and other Near Eastern traditions and used them
in a new way.

As Genesis progresses, this historicised prose fiction[11]
moves steadily away from the motives and habits of the

25

world of legend and myth. While elements of myth remain, the Hebrew scribes seek to affirm that God is present through the experiences of individuals and though the community, and that God makes covenants with the people of Israel.

In describing a god distinct from other ancient Near Eastern deities, who were violent, hierarchical and sexist, Genesis 1:1-2:4a, takes a radically new approach to creation. It can be misinterpreted if taken out of this context. Modern critiques of Genesis 1 focus on the transcendence of God and on the dominion given to human beings. However, when Genesis 1 is read in relation both to the context out of which it developed, and to Genesis 2 and 3, this critique of hierarchy and separateness is moderated.

The genius of the Hebrew Bible is its placing of seemingly contradictory materials side by side, with the expectation that, to see the complete picture, all parts must be taken into account. The parts do not fit perfectly, but the writers were not committed to producing a totally rational text in which all the elements had a logical place. Some nineteenth and twentieth century critics have suggested that the final editors of the biblical text were not aware of the conflicts, but the sophisticated nature of the text suggests otherwise. Like these early writers, we seek to know God, but questions still remain,[12] and our attempts to express our beliefs may not fill the needs of readers two to three thousand years from now. Today, scientists still seek to answer questions about the first moments in time, and have worked back to 10^{-35} of a second following the 'big bang'. Others call on us to own the 'universe story', suggesting that the scientific story of creation has its own power to move and inspire us.[13]

> In the beginning when GOD created the heavens and the earth the earth was a formless void and darkness covered the face of the deep, while a wind from God swept over the face of the waters.
>
> *Genesis 1:1-2*

These verses are an introductory statement, a heading which is unique in ancient Near Eastern literature.[14] The Hebrew text does not speak of the creation of heaven and earth as two separate entities, but as one whole, for there is no single Hebrew word for *cosmos*. The Hebrew *tohu va-bohu* translates into 'formless void'; *tohu* is related to Tiamat.

In later centuries, the integration of Greek thought opened the question of whether there was matter present before God began creation. Augustine, replying to the question of what God did before creation, replied that God was preparing a hell for those who ask that question![15] The classical Christian view was that of creation from nothingness, but the original text does not address this distinction as it does not embody a causal way of thinking. Traditional Jewish theology, followed by Christianity, emphasised creation *ex nihilo* in an effort to demonstrate Yahweh's superiority over, and difference from, Baal, Marduk and other gods. In comparison to Marduk, who needed the corpse of Tiamat to create the world, the author of Genesis 1 emphasises the supreme power of the Creator by omitting any pre-existing elements or other divine beings.

The 'wind from God' is a translation of the Hebrew *ruach*, which, like the Greek *pneuma*, also means 'spirit' or 'breath'. Later rabbinic interpretations visualised the wind as a dove hovering over creation, with clear links to the flood story in Genesis 8:8-12.

A later interpretation of these verses produced the reading:

> In the beginning was the Word, and the Word was with God, and the Word was God. He was in the beginning with God. All things came into being through him, and without him not one thing came into being.
>
> *John 1:1-3a*

John's view of creation seeks to re-interpret Genesis 1 by incorporating Jesus as the Word into the Godhead. The Holy Spirit, seen as a dove, completes the Trinity (John 1:32). The distancing of the Creator of Genesis is now balanced by Jesus as *Emmanuel*, which means 'God with us'.

Early Friends took these verses literally, 'The word of the Lord is that which was in the beginning, and brings to the beginning.'[16] Hence, the Bible could not be the word of God, because Jesus Christ was the Word of God.

The emphasis on creation through the spoken word contrasts with other creation myths which involve sexual activity and an earth-mother. This has led to the unfortunate counter-understanding of the Creator as a distant sky-father. Our experience is of a world in which birth is from a female body. In Genesis 1 we have a detached, painless birthing and an absence of nurturing parenting. When the second creation account, from Genesis 2-3, with its birth of a woman from the side of a man, is added to the first, we have inherited a tradition which, in its attempt to challenge other mythological statements, has created just as many problems as the priestly author was trying to overcome.

❅ ❅ ❅

The stately progression of the text of Genesis 1 parallels the stately progression of creation, a transformation of the violent struggle between chaos and order in other myths: between Marduk and Tiamat in Babylon; Baal whose fight with Yamm (the Mediterranean Sea) confirmed his supremacy in Canaan; and Ra's nightly battle with the chaotic darkness of Nun in Egypt. Genesis 1 projects a powerful, controlled and unemotional god, but other earlier parts of the biblical text repeat the imagery of conflict between order and chaos prevalent in ancient Near Eastern culture.

The prophets, who were writing before the composition of Genesis 1, used the common Near Eastern conflict imagery to represent Yahweh's opposition to countries and kings who were hostile to Yahweh's divine will and purpose:

> Thus says the Lord God:
> I am against you, Pharaoh, king of Egypt,
> the great dragon sprawling in the midst of its channels,
> saying, 'My Nile is my own; I made it for myself.'
> *Ezekiel 29:3*

Mythological imagery serves as evidence of Yahweh's power that can be invoked by the community in the Psalms:

> You divided the sea by your might;
> You broke the heads of the dragons in the waters.
> You crushed the heads of Leviathan;
> You gave him as food for the creatures of the wilderness.
> *Psalm 74:13-14*

Job frequently refers to the mythological conflict, attesting to the power of God over the frailty and limitations of human beings (Job 3:8, 9:8,13, 26:11-13, 38:8-11, 41:1).

In contrast, cosmic creation in Genesis 1 is presented as an orderly progression rather than as a violent struggle. Struggle is focused instead in the Exodus event when the Israelites emerged from slavery in Egypt. The author of Genesis 1 used this as background for his own story:

> The LORD drove the sea back by a strong east wind all night, and turned the sea into dry land; and the waters were divided.
>
> *Exodus 14:21*

This was the decisive time of bringing order out of chaos for the Israelites/Jews, when Yahweh conquered Pharaoh, the god of the Egyptians (Exodus 14:1-15:21).

'Thus the LORD saved Israel that day,' (Exodus 14:30), led to the use of the phrase 'on that day' for other battles, and was projected into the future to introduce the promise of Yahweh's total victory:

> On that day the LORD with his strong and cruel and great sword will punish Leviathan the fleeing serpent, Leviathan the twisting serpent, and he will kill the dragon that is in the sea.
>
> *Isaiah 27:1*

The synoptic gospels and Revelation continue the imagery of cosmic conflict. In a story beginning 'on that day' Jesus rebukes the wind and controls the sea in Mark 4:39. As only God had the authority and power of rebuke in the Hebrew scriptures, early readers recognised the divine power of Jesus in these actions. Jesus also rebukes unclean spirits and Satan, who all represented chaos. Jesus' walking on the sea (Mark 6:45-52) parallels Job's experience of God:

> Who alone stretched out the heavens
> and trampled the waves of the Sea;
> (*or* the back of the sea dragon)
>
> *Job 9:8*

Revelation wallows in apocalyptic imagery,[17] describing a cosmic battle between the forces of order and those of chaos.

Seven angels blow seven trumpets as the Lamb (symbolising Christ) receives a book with seven seals and proceeds to open it. Six of the trumpet blasts unleash disasters on the earth, each of which is the undoing of an act of creation: burning the earth, trees and grass (8:7); polluting the sea with the death of sea creatures (8:9); the pollution of fresh water, causing death (8:10); the destruction of sun, moon and stars, causing day and night to be darkened (8:12); locusts killing all those who do not follow God (9:4) and angels with swords killing most of the remaining human beings (9:13). Victory results in the acclamation of the reign of God and the vision of a new creation (21:1). In the view of the writer of Revelation, creation which was designated 'good' in Genesis 1 has been so corrupted that it has to be destroyed and replaced with a heavenly city.

Civil war broke out in England in 1642 when George Fox was eighteen. This experience of turmoil stimulated the emergence of many radical sects and groups whose religious experience was expressed in apocalyptic language. Religion was the idiom in which people of the seventeenth century thought.[18] Early Friends delighted in the links between the creation stories, Jesus Christ and the book of Revelation. Fox's claim that Christ has come to teach his people himself,[19] challenged the whole life experience of his listeners in terms of authority, politics, religion, economics, and social structures.

George Fox experienced the power of Christ over the elements, 'Never heed the raging waves of the sea,'[20] and he found a rich source of metaphor in the book of Revelation. He experienced the power of the Lord not only as a future hope, but as present reality, 'I had great openings concerning the things written in the Revelations; and when I spoke of them, the priests and professors would say that it was a sealed-up book, and would have kept me out of it.'[21] For Fox, our role in creation is that of the original human beings, part of creation, but responsible to God for creation.

❊ ❊ ❊

The first act of creation, in verse 3, takes the form of a command followed by its execution, 'Then God said, "Let there be light"; and there was light,' a pattern which will be repeated during subsequent days.

Light is the first of many things which are created by God, in clear contrast with the many gods of light, including Ra in Egypt and Mazda in Persia. The creation of light is separate from the creation of the sun, moon and stars in verses 14-16, again emphasising the creative power of God and the created status of these bodies. Early Friends, like Paul in 2 Corinthians 4:6, equated the light with Jesus Christ, '"I am the light of the world, which doth enlighten every man that cometh into the world", saith Christ... This is the light which shows you the evil actions you have all acted... now if you attend to the light it will let you see all that you have done contrary to it; and loving it, it will turn you away from your evil deeds.'[22]

Naming makes it possible to differentiate, to structure and to order. It also implies a sense of power which can be misused as domination. God begins the process of naming by calling the light Day and the darkness Night in verse 5. There is no indication that God created the darkness. Darkness is incorporated into creation.

The ancient Near East viewed the earth as a flat disk surrounded by waters. The dome or firmament prevented the waters above the earth from overwhelming the dry land. In the dome hung the sun, moon and stars. Windows allowed the rain to pass through. The fear that God might

allow the firmament to collapse and engulf the world, was real and ongoing.

Modern readers often reject this account of creation as being unscientific, but this should not diminish its value. In a letter to a family member, the German theologian Karl Barth wrote, 'one can as little compare the biblical creation story and a scientific theory like that of evolution as one can compare, shall we say, an organ and a vacuum cleaner'.[23] While it is non-scientific, the Bible is not anti-scientific. As the dualism between arts and science breaks down, many scientists are reappropriating the stories in the Bible for the deeper truths they reveal: quantum theory looks at possibilities rather than certainties, for example.

The first three days of creation see the separation of light from darkness (verses 3-5); sky from water (verses 6-8); land from sea, and on the land the growth of vegetation (verses 9-13). The next three days parallel the first three: on the fourth day, lights in the sky are created for the night and day (verses 14-18); on the fifth day, birds and fish appear in the water and air (verses 20-23); and on the sixth day animals and humankind are created on the earth (verses 24-27).

Day 1 - light and darkness	Day 4 - sun, moon and stars
Day 2 - sky and water	Day 5 - birds and water creatures
Day 3 - land and seas	Day 6 - land creatures and humankind

It is not a coincidence that the order of creation which occurs over a six day period parallels the order of creation in the *Enuma Elish.* In this earlier account a series of generations of gods is created: gods of water, silt and sky, followed by the heavenly gods, moon, sun and stars.

Each day's work is 'good' (Genesis 1:4,10,12,18,21,24). *Tov*, 'good', also means 'beautiful'. Creation has a quality of beauty which early Friends avoided. Like the Puritans they over-reacted to the excesses of both the wealthy and of Catholicism. Beauty is not frivolous, but is integral to all aspects of life. Margaret Fell challenged the rigid emphasis on plainness when she spoke out for the freedom of the gospel, 'we must look at no colours, nor make anything that is changeable colours as the hills are, nor sell them: but we must all be in one dress and one colour: this is a silly poor Gospel.'[24]

George Fox's experience reflects the goodness of creation:

He is the living God, that clothes the earth with grass and herbs, causes the trees to grow and bring forth food for you and makes the fish of the sea to breathe and live. [He] makes the fowls of the air to breed and causes the roe and the hind, the creatures and the beasts of the earth to bring forth, whereby they may be food for you. He is the living God, that causes the sun to give warmth unto you, to nourish you when you are cold. He is the living God, that causes the snow and the frost to melt and causes the rain to water the plants. He is the living God, that made the heaven and the earth, the clouds, causes the springs to break out of the rocks and divided the great sea from the earth. [He] divides the light from the darkness, by which it is called day and the darkness night, and divided the great waters from the earth, gathered them together, which great waters he called sea and the dry land earth. He is to be worshipped that does this. He is the living God that gives unto you breath, life and strength and gives unto you beasts and cattle, whereby you may be fed and clothed. He is the living God and he is to be worshipped... [25]

✳   ✳   ✳

In the text so far, God has been designated as a single entity. But verses 26 and 27 indicate a plurality, used either as the royal 'we', or more likely to indicate that only in its plurality can humankind reflect God's image:

Then God said, 'Let us make humankind in our image, according to our likeness; and let them have domin- ion over the fish of the sea, and over the birds of the air, and over the cattle, and over all the wild animals of the earth, and over every creeping thing that creeps upon the earth.'

Genesis 1:26

A life-size statue inscribed as the 'image and likeness' of the Assyrian king Hadad-yis'i is the only other known example of these terms being linked together.[26] The Jews forbad the making and worship of idols; God was not known through statues but through created beings.

'In our image' does not refer to a quality of humankind, but to a relationship with God. This makes us responsible to creation when we act as God's counterpart, rather than being set above creation.

The creatures have been differentiated by kind, but not by gender, nor have they been linked to God. Now a new element of creation is introduced:

So God created humankind in His image,
in the image of God He created them;
male and female He created them.

Genesis 1:27

Men and women are created equally. Both sexes are needed to image God. We, as humankind, in all our plurality, are created in God's image. No one of us is created in God's image, but together, with all our colours, shapes and languages, God is imaged. This was a remarkable idea when it was first written, and since that time human beings have tended to emphasise why others are to be excluded rather than to be included in any group. When all are included, relationship takes on a new meaning. The essence of our humanity is in its relatedness. When our relationships are loving, we mirror God's love.

God shares likeness by sharing dominion with humankind who are in healthy relationships with each other.

This is a responsibility not a power trip. Jewish philosopher Abraham Heschel recognised that 'God created a reminder, an image. Humankind is a reminder of God. As God is compassionate, let humanity be compassionate.'[27]

Jesus challenges us to take our responsibility seriously: 'From everyone to whom much has been given, much will be required' (Luke 12:48). We are beginning to recognise that this extends beyond relationships with each other to relationships with all of creation. As our awareness sharpens, we are still unable to discern whether other elements on Earth, abiotic and biotic, have either the need or the capacity to understand that relationship. We are realising that human beings are the creatures who have not been coexisting in a healthy way with the rest of creation. Can we learn?

For George Fox the advent of Jesus was the opportunity for the restoration of this relationship, an opportunity lost, but now restored. 'And when Christ came, he renewed man into the image of God again, and unto his law, but since the apostles' day have they lost his image of God and this likeness... but now is Christ renewing man again into the image of God.'[28]

A current interpreter, Stephen Hawking, has said, 'I think computer viruses should count as life... I think it says something about human nature that the only form of life we have created so far is purely destructive. We've created life in our own image'.[29]

Genesis 1 presents a unique relationship between God and human beings, with God giving over power of governance and human beings becoming the agents to whom much is given and from whom much expected. There is both closeness and distance in the relationship between God and human beings. Closeness is the trust given to humankind; distance allows human beings to have the freedom of response to God.

God blesses the human beings and, in singling them out to 'be fruitful and multiply', blesses their sexual relationship. If we can let go of the negative interpretations of many Christian theologians, who used this verse to stigmatise homosexual relationships, we may be able to look at the text as it stands, an affirmation of the creation of new life. God's good creation continues.

✳ ✳ ✳

The words 'dominion' and 'subdue' are stumbling blocks to many modern readers:

> 'God blessed them, and God said to them, "Be fruitful and multiply, and fill the earth and subdue it; and have dominion over the fish of the sea and over the birds of the air and over every living thing that moves upon the earth."'

Genesis 1:28

In its original context the text sought to emphasise that human beings were not slaves to the destructive whims of the gods, but had a specific role in creation. This has left later generations with the challenge of an appropriate interpretation of 'dominion'. *Qabash* (subdue) comes from a Hebrew root meaning 'to tread down' and *radah* (dominion) conveys an image of treading or trampling, an attitude observed by T. H. White, 'Our approach to nature is to beat it into submission. We would stand a better chance of survival if we accommodated ourselves to this planet and viewed it appreciatively, instead of sceptically and dictatorially.'[30]

Gerald Wilson provides an alternate interpretation of these words when used in the biblical text, suggesting that the emphasis is on the exercise of authority.[31] Humankind is given authority over the creatures, but is itself still subject to God's authority.

The dominion mandated here refers to the whole of creation, but focuses on the animals. Dominance is that of a shepherd who cares for sheep. Ezekiel castigates shepherds who abuse this responsibility:

> Should not shepherds feed the sheep? You eat the fat, you clothe yourselves with the wool, you slaughter the fatlings; but you do not feed the sheep. You have not strengthened the weak, you have not healed the sick, you have not bound up the injured, you have not brought back the strayed, you have not sought the lost, but with force and harshness you have ruled them.
>
> *Ezekiel 34:2-4*

Jesus tells the parable of a manager, put in charge of his master's slaves, which ends with the warning:

> . . . From everyone to whom much has been given, much will be required; and from the one to whom much has been entrusted, even more will be demanded.
>
> *Luke 12:48*

In recent centuries we have used Genesis 1:26-28 to justify our dominion over the earth, but have missed a fuller understanding of the biblical record. Image and dominion find resolution and convergence in Jesus, who is portrayed as the good shepherd (John 10:11). As a human being he chose to reveal his spiritual inheritance in his way of life and acceptance of death.

George Fox was comfortable with the word 'dominion', using it for the relationship intended between humankind who 'dwell in the light'[32] and the creatures: 'when God Almighty had made and created all things, he saw that they were good, yea, very good, and blessed them; and made man and woman in his own image and likeness, and set them in dominion above all that he made, and they were made good and perfect and he blessed them.'[33] Even as an eleven year old he challenged those who devoured creation,[34] and later, in a 'warning to the people of England', he chastised those who 'waste the creatures of God.'[35]

✳ ✳ ✳

After dealing differently with human beings than with the other elements of creation, by speaking to them and giving them dominion over the animals, God reminds them of their link to creation, the need for nourishment,

> God said, 'See, I have given you every plant yielding seed that is upon the face of all the earth, and every tree with seed in its fruit; you shall have them for food. And to every beast of the earth, and to every bird of the air, and to everything that creeps on the earth, everything that has the breath of life, I have given every green plant for food.' And it was so.

> *Genesis 1:29-30*

Human beings are to eat the seed and the fruit of plants while animals eat the leaves. The author suggests that there is no need for living creatures to deprive each other of life in order to live. The killing of animals for meat was centred on the sacrificial system as a means of handling guilt. Killing animals was part of dealing with the disorder of life, and the author looked to an ideal in which there was no place for slaughter. At a time when God saw that everything was good, killing animals was unnecessary.

The interdependence of all of creation is very apparent in this story. Many of us have lost conscious awareness of this.

We do not realise that the elements that make up our bodies have circulated through other beings for the 4,500,000,000 years of Earth's evolution. The water, carbon and nitrogen cycles we see on the pages of school science books are part of who we are, as are the food chains and the cycle of production, consumption and decomposition.

Plants use only one percent of the light energy they receive, herbivores use ten percent of the energy they ingest and carnivores use a further ten percent. Each stage of the food chain depends on a much larger supply base. Meat eating for most of human life has been the special food of festivals, not the staple diet.[36] Can we learn from this?

✳ ✳ ✳

The climax of creation is the seventh day, when God rested,

> And on the seventh day God finished the work that he had done, and he rested on the seventh day from all the work that he had done. So God blessed the seventh day and hallowed it, because on it God rested from all the work that he had done in creation.
>
> *Genesis 2:2-3*

This is in sharp contrast to the climax of the Babylonian creation story which is the public glorification of Marduk as all the gods proclaim his honour. Creation is patterned after the week which the author intended to be normative for the community; one of six days' work followed by the sabbath, a sabbath in total contrast to the primordial chaos that preceded the first day.

God said that each creative act was 'good', but the first thing to be made 'holy' was the seventh day (Genesis 2:3). This is the only such designation in the creation accounts. Two other aspects of creation are named holy in the Hebrew scriptures: the ground around the burning bush (Exodus 3:5), and the people of Israel (Exodus 19:6). Time, place and creatures are holy.

The land was part of the covenant relationship between God and Israel. Care for the land maintained the covenant and destruction of the land broke the relationship with God: 'the land will vomit you out for defiling it' (Leviticus 18:28). Sabbatical legislation incorporates a series of cycles, seven days, seven years, and seven times seven years. This calendric legislation involves both the land and the people.

Early Sabbaths were celebrated with time away from work for human beings and their animals, and with occasional festal activities. About two hundred years before Jesus's birth, pious Jews would not defend themselves on the Sabbath and were massacred by the Seleucids.[37] Jews were not conscripted into the Roman army because of this respect for the Sabbath. The Pharisees devised regulations to protect the Sabbath,[38] and Jesus's ministry reflects his rejection of these barriers to an intimacy with God and creation.

The Israelites were to give the land sabbatical rest:

> When you enter the land that I am giving you, the land shall observe a sabbath to the LORD. Six years you shall sow your field, and six years you shall prune your vineyard, and gather in their yield; but in the seventh year there shall be a sabbath of complete rest for the land, a sabbath for the LORD: you shall not sow your field or prune your vineyard... for your livestock also, and for the wild animals in your land all its yield shall be for food.
> *Leviticus 25:2-4,7*

Radical trust, radical rest for creation. A letting go by human beings of the need to control, covet and own. Other conditions of the sabbatical year were the option of freedom for all slaves (Deuteronomy 15:12-14), access by the poor to all farm lands and crops (Exodus 23:11), and the cancellation of all debts (Deuteronomy 15:1-2).

Every fiftieth year, there was an even greater commitment to trust in God, the year of Jubilee:

> And you shall hallow the fiftieth year, and proclaim liberty throughout the land to all its inhabitants. It shall be a jubilee for you: you shall return, every one of you, to your property and every one you to your family. That fiftieth year shall be a jubilee for you: you shall not sow, or reap the aftergrowth, or harvest the unpruned vine... The land shall not be sold in perpetuity, for the land is mine; with me you are but aliens and tenants.
>
> *Leviticus 25:10-11,23*

In the time of Jeremiah, King Zedekiah released all the slaves, but immediately returned them to slavery. As a result, he received the brunt of one of Jeremiah's prophetic utterances (Jeremiah 34).

Jesus' ministry was based on the celebration of Jubilee. When he re-interpreted Isaiah 60:1-2a in the synagogue at Nazareth, he re-affirmed Jubilee, the 'year of the Lord's favour', and along with it a ministry which reflected God's will for the people: a people who are freed from bondage, whose poor receive good news, whose prisoners are freed and whose sick are healed. Jesus did not speak directly of leaving the soil fallow, perhaps because this was the one aspect of sabbatical observance that was regularly observed. He also spoke out against a law which was designed to avoid the need to forgive debts by transferring the right of recovery to a court (Matthew 15:5-9).

The book of Leviticus responds to questions about the sufficiency of food in the rest year:

> Should you ask, 'What shall we eat in the seventh year, if we may not sow or gather in our crop?' I will order my blessing for you in the sixth year, so that it will yield a crop for three years.
>
> *Leviticus 25:20-21*

Jesus uses similar words when speaking to the disciples. The proclamation of Jubilee may have troubled them because they left their fields untilled and their boats at the lakeshore to follow him:

> Do not be worry about your life, what you will eat, or about your body, what you will wear... strive for God's kingdom, and these things shall be given to you as well.
>
> *Luke 12:22,31*

Jubilee may not have been celebrated fully, for the trust needed is not easily built. The idea, though, presents a model for us in our life on this planet. It does not rely on an apocalyptic scenario of supernatural events to purge the world of evil. It recognises that relationships degenerate between human beings, animals and the earth, and that these need periodic correction, so that creation can begin afresh. Cancellation of debts to the two-third-world nations is a small beginning, but, until we take responsibility for relationships closer to home, we are not living in a state of radical trust.

Friends' testimony on days and times affirms that the secular should be raised up to the sacred, and that all times have the quality of Sabbath, a positive rather than a negative affirmation. John Luffe was one of the Friends who travelled with Mary Fisher. In discussion with Pope Alexander VII, about 1658, he said, ' "Every day is a Sabbath wherein we can serve God." The Pope responded, "Very well, and is there nothing to be done for the remembrance' sake of our

Saviour's blessed ascension?" "No, no, I have Christ about me and in me, and therefore cannot choose but remember him continually".'[39]

In this late twentieth century world we seem to be driven by external factors, like machines in a factory. We need to reject the pressure to produce and consume. We seem to oscillate between driven achievement and mind-numbing private escape which between them increasingly poison our institutions, relationships, quality of life and the creation around us.

Where in this scenario do we find Sabbath time, a time that can *ground* us, a sane and holy rhythm of life?

Technology is often blamed for the quality of life which first-world people experience. Most of today's technology is prescriptive and results in the division of labour and specialization by process, encouraging a culture of compliance in which machines are trusted over human beings. Redemptive technology incorporates different values in its development: promoting justice, restoring reciprocity, conferring benefits, preferring people to machines, maximizing gain and minimizing disaster, favouring conservation over waste and reversible decisions over irreversible ones.[40] Redemptive technology can release us from our self-imposed treadmills to discover Sabbath time.

Sabbath time is not just a one-day-a-week experience, but can spill over into each and every day, as experienced by Thomas Kelly:

> Begin where you are. Obey *now*. Use what little obedience you are capable of, even if it be like a grain of mustard seed. Begin where you are. Live this present moment, this present hour as you now sit in your seats, in utter, utter submission and openness toward Him. Listen outwardly to these words, but within, behind the

> scenes, in the deeper levels of your lives where you are
> alone with God the Loving Eternal One, keep up a silent
> prayer 'Open thou my life. Guide my thoughts where I
> dare not let them go. But thou darest. Thy will be done'...
> ... Don't grit your teeth and clench your fists and say, 'I
> will! I will!' Relax. Take hands off. Submit yourself to
> God. Learn to live in the passive voice - a hard saying for
> Americans - and let life be willed through you'.[41]

Stopping work totally requires trust. Will the world fall
apart if I stop making things happen for a while? In the
desert, God told the Israelites to pick only enough manna for
each day; extra food rotted. On the sixth day an extra
quantity was picked which stayed fresh for the Sabbath.
Trust was needed to discover the rhythm of God's provi-
dence.

Thomas Merton quotes Douglas Steere:

> There is a pervasive form of contemporary violence to
> which the idealist fighting for peace by nonviolent meth-
> ods most easily succumbs: activism and overwork. The
> rush and pressure of modern life are a form, perhaps the
> most common form, of its innate violence. To allow
> oneself to be carried away by a multitude of conflicting
> concerns, to surrender to too many demands, to commit
> oneself to too many projects, to want to help everyone in
> everything is to succumb to violence. More than that it is
> cooperation with violence.[42]

Where is Sabbath time in this? How many of us recognise
ourselves in this scenario?

Although Genesis 1, positioned at the opening of the Bible,
might seem to set the tone for the ongoing story of creation,
we have seen that other, older texts contain elements of Near
Eastern traditions, indicating the continuing influence these

traditions had in the lives of the Israelites, and later the Jews. The bold attempt of the priestly writer to set a context in which the Hebrew scriptures could be viewed seems not to have been successful.

As educated, late-twentieth-century individuals, we may try to deny the power and influence of myth in our lives. The priestly writers were well aware of the power of myth and sought to replace the Babylonian understanding of creation with their elegant unfolding of order. Unfortunately, the struggle between order and chaos still echoes throughout the biblical text.

Paul Ricoeur identified the continuing Babylonian heritage as contributing to the theology of war,[43] in which we identify the enemy as the powers of chaos which undergirds western culture. This has been called 'the myth of redemptive violence,'[44] in which the survival and welfare of the nation is the greatest good. It is played out in children's cartoons, films, foreign policy and militarism.

'And God saw everything that he had made, and indeed, it was very good' (Genesis 1:31). God's pronouncement on the whole of creation is one we need to own and celebrate. Wonder, renewal, a sense of beauty and the capacity to rejoice are integral to our creatureliness. Shug, in *The Color Purple*, abandons typical God language as she affirms, 'I think it pisses God off if you walk by the color purple in a field somewhere and don't notice it.'[45]

This account of creation ends with the first genealogy of the biblical text, 'These are the generations of the heaven and the earth when they were created' (Genesis 2:4a). Later biblical genealogies list people, compared to genealogies of creation in other Near East myths which list the gods; here creation is the focus with mythology being transformed into theology.

Chapter III

IN THE GARDEN:
GENESIS 2:4B-3:24

FOLLOWING the majestic scope of Genesis 1, Genesis 2:4b-3:24 approaches creation from a very different perspective and introduces a whole new set of challenges. Instead of taking oversight of an orderly creation, God is an experimenter with lots still to learn, and instead of a liturgical text, a tale of alienation between humanity and God takes centre stage. Genesis 1 presented a complete plan for creation, while Genesis 2-3 explores the same ground by examining human beings, their relationships, their potential and their limitations. Repetitions, additions and omissions, which emphasise communication and miscommunication in Genesis 2-3, replace the generative power and the consistency in the use of language of Genesis 1.

Modern explanations might describe the two accounts as products of left and right brain thought or arising from a 'he said, she said' perspective. The tensions between the accounts are an example of how the Bible speaks with multiple voices, like a '"gathered meeting" focused and yet diverse in the perspectives by which a theme is addressed, each message to be seasoned in dialogue with the others'.[1]

No text in Genesis has been more used, interpreted and misunderstood than Genesis 2-3. It is seen as:

- a foundational text for the Bible, but within the biblical literature itself it is rarely mentioned.

- an account of 'the fall', but Hosea, Jeremiah and Ezekiel are more dogmatic in presenting a negative view of human nature. Not until 2 Esdras 7:118 and Romans 5:14[2] is a connection made between the sin of Adam and Eve and that of all human beings made, a connection that later developed into the doctrine of original sin.

- an explanation of how evil entered creation, although the Bible offers no statement about the origin of evil and does not address such abstract issues.

- an account of the origin of death, yet the Bible typically sees death as part of human life.

- a highlighting of the evils of sex, though Genesis 2-3 examines the dynamics of power, control and autonomy.[3]

It is difficult to approach Genesis 2-3 and read it without the inherited interpretations that we assume are part of the text. Even a new reading[4] leaves us with challenges to address, but the exercise can demonstrate how powerful the text and its traditional interpretations are in our lives. During the reformation, when relics were removed from cathedrals, Coventry lost its handful of the dust from which Adam was made. Traditional interpretations may not be disposed of so easily.

Genesis 2-3 has a very different history from Genesis 1. It was probably an oral story that evolved through various forms before being written down between 960 and 920 BCE.[5] The writer may have combined at least two earlier traditions: one which described the creation of human beings, another which gave the reason for human limitations and problems, along with older tales of trees as the symbol of the mother goddess. This is not a naive story for it builds tension as it offers a sophisticated, sustained and intentional reflection on human destiny. It is an account of God calling human beings to be God's creatures, to live in creation on God's terms.

The writer may have been a member of the royal court, writing during the reign of Solomon or his son Rehoboam.[6] The complete text by this author provides an early history for the new kingdom. There was probably little thought that this folksy narrative would become part of a holy book of two world religions. A parallel history of the court, 2 Samuel, was also taking shape during this time.

Scholars use the letter *J* (see appendix) to designate this royal writer, because God is named Yahweh (*Jahveh* in German) throughout the narrative. However, in Genesis 2-3, God is called Yahweh-Elohim,[7] designated by 'LORD God' in the *NRSV*. This may have been a later editorial attempt to make a link between the god of Genesis 1 and the god of Genesis 2-3.

The Israelites needed an official history which incorporated the radical changes which had occurred with the formation of the monarchy. Prior to 1020 BCE they were a loose federation of tribes held together by their experience of the Exodus and their allegiance to the covenant. Their allegiance was reaffirmed in ceremonies centred on the Ark, the mobile repository for the tablets of the ten commandments and other artifacts. Tribes responded locally to threats of aggression as amply recorded in Judges.

The Philistines invaded Egypt from the north at the end of the eleventh century BCE, but were repelled and settled as mercenaries on the Mediterranean coast near Gaza, bringing with them new iron weapons. A monarchy would enable the Israelites to mount a centralized military response to the Philistines.

Any political shift of this significance is accompanied by other changes, including, in this case a radical restructuring of religion. Up to this time polytheism had been widely tolerated. Even the high priest was an active participant in such rituals.[8] The worship of Yahweh was to be the sole faith of the new nation and so religious allegiance was shifted by representing the old symbols as evil.[9]

❈ ❈ ❈

This author, J, introduces only the elements needed to set up the context of the action, and so the story opens with a preface which describes the early stages of creation only briefly:

> In the day that the LORD God made the earth and the heavens, when no plant of the field was yet in the earth and no herb of the field had yet sprung up, for the LORD God had not caused it to rain upon the earth, and there was no one to till the ground ...
>
> *Genesis 2:4b-5*

A subterranean stream, which waters the surface of the ground, eliminates the lifelessness of the earth (Genesis 2:6). Water has a very different role from that of 'the deep' in Genesis 1. The Hebrews knew of the danger of the sea, but had also met the danger of the desert with its daily challenge to find water. Genesis 1 is based on a Babylonian cycle of dry land appearing after winter floods, while Genesis 2 is based on the Canaanite experience of refreshing autumn rains after a summer drought. Such contrasting experiences are expressed dialectically throughout the scriptures.

Two related words used in the Hebrew text are woven into the structure of the story: 'man' (here 'no one') from the NRSV is *adam*, and *ha-adama* is 'the ground'. *Adam* is usually translated into English as 'man', but in this context might better be translated as 'groundling', 'earthling', 'earth creature' or 'Dusty'. This maintains the original pun and leaves a degree of tension about what or who is this element of creation. Unfortunately, the New Revised Standard Version, along with older translations, uses 'man' for both the groundling of Genesis 2:5-22 and the male person of Genesis 2:23 onwards. I will maintain the original distinction between the two creatures.

The role of the groundling is defined as a tiller, Hebrew *bd*, of the earth. This may also be translated as 'server of the earth', for *bd* connotes respect, reverence and worship. This is a very different concept from our perception of 'dominion over the earth' in Genesis 1:26.

God creates the groundling:

> ... then the LORD God formed man from the dust of the ground, and breathed into his nostrils the breath of life; and the man became a living being.
>
> *Genesis 2:7*

Instead of creating by word, the God of Genesis 2 acts as a potter, moulding a creature into whose nostrils God breathes life, *nephesh*. *Nephesh* may be translated as 'living soul', but avoids the Greek tendency of dualism into body and soul, a concept unknown in Hebrew thought. *Nephesh* expresses the total person as body, soul and spirit in a unified whole. It also incorporates the idea of a person in community, in relation to others, for example as parent, friend, teacher or employer.[10]

Human creation from clay is a common motif in ancient Near Eastern literature. In Egypt, either the god Khnum or the god Ptah created a man on a potter's wheel; in Babylonia, either the goddess Aruru or the god Ea kneaded a man from clay. Prometheus used a red clay at Panopeus, from which came the smell of human flesh.[11]

The groundling becomes the focus of God's attention as the story unfolds. During this unfolding, the five senses gradually develop. These are the groundling's contacts with creation. The groundling is not a male person, but is a human being, sexually undifferentiated and dependent on God for further development.

The Babylonians saw primeval man as being androgynous. In the *Epic of Gilgamesh*, dated before 1000 BCE, Enkidu is a wild man who was created from clay. Enkidu lived with gazelles and wild cattle, and swam with dolphins, but had hair like that of a woman. Hunters tricked him by sending him a temple prostitute. After Enkidu had intercourse with her the animals ran from him in fear.[12]

God creates a specific place in which to locate the groundling. Eden is a probable pun on the Hebrew word for 'enjoyment'.

> And the LORD God planted a garden in Eden, in the east; and there he put the man whom he had formed. Out of the ground the LORD God made to grow every tree that is pleasant to the sight and good for food, the tree of life also in the midst of the garden, and the tree of the knowledge of good and evil. A river flows out of Eden to water the garden, and there it divides and becomes four branches... The LORD God took the man and put him in the garden of Eden to till it and keep it.

> *Genesis 2:8-15*

The role of the groundling is confirmed and expanded, 'to till and to keep' the garden, one of the needs of the garden, the other being water, which is also provided by the river. 'Keep', Hebrew *smr*, denotes protection, not possession. The role of the groundling is limited to caring for the garden. There is still no creature to care for the ground outside the garden (Genesis 2:5).

The groundling is not passive but participative. Work is an integral part of the creation of humanity, and of the groundling's relationship to the rest of creation. That relationship is carried out with care and respect.

❋ ❋ ❋

The text mentions two particular trees, the Tree of Life and the tree of the knowledge of good and evil, more literally 'the tree of knowing good and bad'. The Tree of Life was one of the central images of the goddess in Near Eastern religious traditions, a symbol which linked heaven, earth and the underworld. The Babylonian goddess of the Tree of Life was named Edin, 'the Divine Lady of Eden'.[13] To remain immortal, gods and goddesses had to eat the fruit of the tree which was often guarded by serpents. King Sargon of Sumeria was named the beloved gardener of the goddess Ishtar.[14] The Canaanite tradition of men going to sacred groves to receive oracles may be part of the background of this story.

At the time the early versions of this story were developing, the Hebrews were moving from a nomadic culture into one that incorporated horticulture. Tropical fruits from Africa and the East were introduced by caravans.[15] The Tree of Life is not mentioned again until Genesis 3:22.[16]

God offers both choice and boundaries to the groundling:

> And the LORD God commanded the man, 'You may freely eat of every tree of the garden; but of the tree of the knowledge of good and evil you shall not eat, for in the day that you eat of it you shall die.'
>
> *Genesis 2:16-17*

'You may freely eat', are the first words the groundling hears. The link between work and food was very apparent to early societies. Today we spend comparatively little time or money in obtaining food, but deep ecologists remind us there is no such thing as a free lunch.

A limitation balances the freedom of choice. Eating can bring both life and death. While the depths of meaning in the phrase 'knowledge of good and evil' are still not fully understood, it is clearly linked to discernment. God gives the groundling a wide range of choices and one prohibition, but offers little explanation. The groundling has not yet spoken and so cannot question God's statement. The groundling's senses are developing, for now taste, sight and hearing are actively used.

God is presented as an experimenter, a model maker, or a child who adds piece by piece, sometimes randomly, to a world created in a sand box.

> Then the LORD God said, 'It is not good that the man should be alone; I will make him a helper as his partner.' So out of the ground the LORD God formed every animal of the field and every bird of the air, and brought them to the man to see what he would call them; and whatever the man called every living creature, that was its name. The man gave names to all cattle, and to the birds of the air, and to every animal of the field; but for the man there was not found a helper as his partner.
>
> *Genesis 2:18-20*

God is seeking to create a helper and partner for the groundling, a creature in equal relationship with the groundling. 'Helper' is *ezer*, which usually refers to God as a superior who creates and saves Israel. The Hebrew text also has *kenegdo*, 'corresponding to it'. A literal translation gives 'corresponding to partner'. This modifies any implication of superiority by emphasising mutuality and equality.

Animals and birds are formed in a way which is identical to the creation of the groundling. In addition to the role of tilling and keeping, the groundling is given the privilege and power of naming the animals, and therefore acquires speech. Each naming is an encounter with a potential partner.

God has made all the decisions up to this point in creation. The groundling, by naming the animals, becomes part of a process of shared decision-making. But, situated in a verdant garden that is filled with birds and animals, the groundling is still without a partner. The previous verses may be one way of suggesting what the partner is not.

God tries again, but, instead of seeking to create a partner directly from the ground, returns the groundling to the passive state in which the groundling had been before receiving the breath of life. Out of the groundling comes the material for a new creation:

> So the LORD God caused a deep sleep to fall upon the man, and he slept; then he took one of his ribs and closed up its place with flesh. And the rib that the LORD God had taken from the man he made into a woman and brought her to the man.
>
> *Genesis 2:21-22*

Within this account of creation the creation of woman is unique. The groundling, trees, birds and animals had been made from the ground, but the woman was made from the groundling. The intent of the author may have been to focus on the equality of the man and the woman. However, these verses have been used in very different ways. In a male-dominated society this text has be used to support the control of women's bodies by men.

It seems that the woman's ability to create life threatens patriarchal authority, and is an element which still feeds our contemporary struggle over contraception and abortion. The sacrament of baptism, whether of children or of adults, which has been performed only by men for almost 2,000 years, is a further example of the symbolic degradation of birthing by women. Creation occurred without female involvement in Genesis 1, and now this second account sets up a scenario which, with its accompanying patriarchal interpretations, is rightly challenged by today's feminists.

This is not the only Near Eastern story which involves life being created from a rib. The Sumerian word for 'life', *ti*, also meant 'rib'. The Sumerian mother goddess healed the rib of a god by creating Nin-ti, the goddess of childbirth. Nin-ti made the bones of babies in the womb from the ribs of their mothers. Nin-ti means both 'the lady who gives life' and 'the lady of the rib.'[17] In Hebrew there is also a pun on *tsela*, 'rib', but it is a less positive comparison than the Sumerian word play, for its other meaning is 'stumbling'.

In becoming material for creation, the groundling is changed, and the groundling's first direct speech shows that change, despite the *NRSV* translation:

> Then the man said,
> 'This at last is bone of my bones
> and flesh of my flesh;
> this one shall be called Woman,
> for out of Man this one was taken.'
> Therefore a man leaves his father and his mother and
> clings to his wife, and they become one flesh.
>
> *Genesis 2:23-4*

There is continuity between the original groundling and the new man and woman, but also discontinuity. *Ishah*, 'woman' (taken out of man) and *ish*, 'man', are the groundling's identification of the new creatures which have been formed, as the groundling, now a male person, owns the personal change that has occurred. There is not a naming by the new man of the new woman, with its implication of power. This will come later. Their creation has been simultaneous. They are not opposites of each another, but an extension of the original creation which has been further differentiated by God to create equal partners.

Genesis 2:23 is in poetic form. This may suggest the inclusion of an already existing text into the narrative that reflects community expectations at the time of writing. The only other poem in these early chapters is in Genesis 1:27. Both refer to human essence defined in relationship to a partner and to God. Verse 24 may also reflect a statement of the community at the time of writing.

> And the man and his wife were both naked, and were not ashamed.
>
> *Genesis 2:25*

Since the couple have been created by God they have nothing to hide, and nakedness is not a problem. God created human beings who are sexually differentiated. Sexuality expresses God's intention that authentic humanness is found in relationship. They have choices and they live in a place that can nurture them and give them pleasure. They are not absolute individuals, but are in community, and as such have responsibilities, including those to the environment.

While Genesis 1 portrayed human sex in terms of reproduction, Genesis 2 focuses on pleasure and beauty in commitment to each other. Being naked is being defenceless and vulnerable to the other.

George Fox's understanding of this verse led him to establish men's and women's meetings. This was done at a time when many Friends were being imprisoned, and illustrates Fox's clear vision of a restored community.[18] This restoration aimed to 'admonish, and exhort such as walked disorderly or carelessly, and not according to Truth; and to take care of God's glory.'[19] He wrote an epistle to 'All your Men's and Women's meetings everywhere, keep in the Power of the Lord Jesus Christ in his Gospel... help-meets in the Restoration as Man and Woman was before the Fall in the Garden of God.'[20]

This stage in J's story of creation is reflected in many ways by Isaiah's vision of the peaceable kingdom:

> The wolf shall live with the lamb,
> the leopard shall lie down with the kid,
> the calf and the lion and the fatling together,
> and a little child shall lead them.
> The cow and the bear shall graze,
> their young shall lie down together;
> and the lion shall eat straw like the ox.
> The nursing child shall play over the hole of the asp,
> and the weaned child shall put its hand on the adder's den.
> They will not hurt or destroy on all My holy mountain
> *Isaiah 11:6-9a*

Bountiful nature is a backdrop to animals and human beings living in harmony, *shalom*. Relationships are open, balanced and healthy. The man and woman still exhibit the childlike innocence of the children in Isaiah's vision.

During the Orthodox-Hicksite controversy in the nineteenth century, American Quaker Edward Hicks created a series of paintings depicting the peaceable kingdom. In each foreground the various animals are grouped in a literal representation of Isaiah's prophecy. However, in the background, details change over time. In early paintings, William Penn's treaty with the Indians forms the background. This is later replaced by a pyramid of Friends carrying banners. In the forefront of the group is Elias Hicks, Edward's cousin, 'the storm center of the conflict.'[21] At the end of Genesis 2, we wonder what is happening in the background to threaten this ideal existence.

❊　❊　❊

A new character enters the story in chapter 3, introduced by a pun which links the serpent to the couple: *arum*, 'subtle', counterbalances *arom*, 'naked'. 'Shrewd' and 'nude' convey the word play in English.

> Now the serpent was more subtle than any other wild animal that the LORD God had made. He said to the woman, 'Did God say, "You shall not eat from any tree in the garden"?' The woman said to the serpent, 'We may eat of the fruit of the trees in the garden; but God said, "You shall not eat of the fruit of the tree that is in the middle of the garden, nor shall you touch it, or you shall die."'
>
> *Genesis 3:1-3*

When the serpent addresses the woman it speaks to her in the plural form, as though addressing both man and woman. The serpent and the woman discuss theology. They do not use the name 'Yahweh' in discussing God, but employ the more general term 'Elohim', distancing themselves from the close relationship established by 'Yahweh-Elohim'. This is a conversation introduced with deliberate half-truths. The serpent's question, 'Did God say, "You shall not eat from any tree in the garden"?' needs an answer beyond a simple 'Yes' or 'No'. The woman's answer restates God's original instructions and she speaks for herself and for the man. She changes 'the tree of the knowledge of good and evil' to 'the tree that is in the middle of the garden' and adds the prohibition of touching the tree. With this reference to touch, all five senses have been invoked in the story. This additional prohibition indicates that the original warning had been heard and had been fully understood. To touch brings one close to disobedience. Staying well away may prevent temptation.

The serpent challenges God's declaration:

> But the serpent said to the woman, 'You will not die; for God knows that when you eat of it your eyes will be opened, and you will be like God, knowing good and evil.'

Genesis 3:4-5

How will the woman respond to the serpent's assertion that instead of death, as promised by God, the results of eating will be in being God-like?

For over a thousand years before Genesis 2-3 took shape, the Tree of Life, symbol of the mother goddess, was also linked with the serpent. The serpent could be guardian of the tree, adornment for, or consort of the goddess.[22]

The ability of snakes to appear silently in the spring after a hard winter, and the practice of shedding their skin, associated them with rejuvenation and regeneration. The serpent also acquired the reputation of having a dual nature, being capable of both good and evil. It was pictured standing erect when good, but crawled when it was evil.[23]

In the biblical record the serpent also takes on a range of characteristics. Here it is sly. In the story of the Exodus, Moses' rod turns into serpents to convince the Hebrews of God's presence (Exodus 4:3). Later, Moses sets up a brazen serpent to heal those bitten by serpents (Numbers 21:6, 8-9). The brass serpent was placed in the Ark of the Covenant which eventually was lodged in the Holy of Holies in the Jerusalem Temple until it was removed about 700 BCE by King Hezekiah (2 Kings 18:4). Jesus sends out his disciples with the injunctions that they be 'wise as serpents, harmless as doves' (Matthew 10:16). A direct link is made between Satan, dragon and serpent in Revelation 12:9 and 20:2.

Early Friends associated the serpent with the devil. They called the serpent the 'world's god'[24] who held people in a sinful state, against whom Jesus Christ was victorious.

The motives of the serpent in this story are not made clear. Perhaps it wanted to be a companion to the groundling but was passed over. Perhaps it disliked not being centre stage like the man and woman. Or perhaps it was a casualty of the ideological battle being fought to replace the goddess and her consort with the very singular Yahweh.

The serpent had power, power to cause the woman and man to question the relationship which God had established. Symbolically, the animal world challenged both human and divine spheres by using the plant world.

One can infer from the text that the man was a passive witness to the encounter between the serpent and the woman. George Fox understands the serpent's approach to the woman to include the man: 'the serpent (did) make his text of to beguile and deceive man and woman with, which God had forbidden man and woman to eat of. And he being more subtile than any beast of the field, he said to the woman ... '[25]

> So when the woman saw that the tree was good for food, and that it was a delight to the eyes, and that the tree was to be desired to make one wise, she took of its fruit and ate;
>
> *Genesis 3:6a*

Without consulting the man, who is with her, the woman eats the fruit from the tree as she seeks the promised wisdom. The woman does not die. The serpent was right!

> ... and she also gave some to her husband, who was with her, and he ate. Then the eyes of both were opened, and

they knew that they were naked; and they sewed fig
leaves together and made loincloths for themselves.

Genesis 3:6b-7

She offers the fruit to the man, who accepts it without
question. Taking, eating, and giving become actions that
change for the worse the relationship between human beings
and God. The same three actions will restore the relationship
between human beings and God at the last supper.

The woman has been an active participant in the conversation with the serpent, in choosing to eat and in sharing the
fruit with the man. The text does not imply that the man was
actively tempted by the woman, but that he passively observed the conversation and accepted the proffered fruit
without question. There is no indication of what type of
fruit was involved.[26]

The temptations of Jesus parallel those of the man and the
woman. The woman knew that the tree was good for food
and the devil tempts Jesus with bread; the fruit was a
delight to the eyes and Jesus was shown all the kingdoms of
the world but chose to work in the spiritual realm; eating
from the tree gave divine power but Jesus rejected the
temptation of power in Luke 4:1-13.

In *Women's Speaking Justified*, Margaret Fell suggests that
the serpent approached the woman because of 'his subtlety
discerning her to be the weaker vessel, or more inclinable to
hearken to him'. Her response to the punishment of enmity
between the seeds of the serpent and the woman is that
women must speak out or only the voice of the serpent will
be heard.[27]

There are two ways of knowing for George Fox, inward and outward,[28] and he uses this metaphor to interpret
these verses, 'So man did eat: the eye out, the ear out, at last
the mouth out too.'[29] The inward Spirit of Christ gives true

knowledge, but the senses can be misled by outer knowledge. Fox believed that the hearing and obeying relationship has been lost and now 'all stand naked and bare before the living God. For woe is to everyone, that is covered, but not with the spirit of the Lord.'[30] Fox sees the making of clothes from fig leaves as the origin of 'pride, haughtiness, high-mindedness, and the abominable customs and fashions, and the ungodly lusts of the world', resulting from 'forsaking the Lord's teaching, and following the Serpent's.'[31]

Puritans eliminated the dangers of the senses by restricting colour, music and other pleasures from daily life and worship. The ear was the main organ for experiencing God. The word, through scripture and sermon was the most trustworthy vehicle. Sight, touch, smell and taste were unreliable. Friends were not immune to this culture.

❋ ❋ ❋

From an ideal relationship at the end of chapter 2, we now have a fearful couple whose knowledge has not given them wisdom. Their one flesh is separated. Their eyes have been opened, as the serpent promised, but they are not like God. The man and woman act like frightened children, not like god-like beings. Clothes cover not only their bodies, but also their helplessness and insecurity. They 'came to be dead to God; and instead of being wiser, came to be fools'.[32] Fig leaves feel like sandpaper at certain points in their growth, a point probably not lost to early audiences. The sycamore fig, a large-leaved variety, was sacred to the goddess Asherah in Canaan.

Anxiety is a new experience for the man and the woman: anxiety to eat the fruit, anxiety about their nakedness, anxiety about meeting God. Jesus calls on people not to worry, Matthew 6:25-34, but to live in a state of Sabbath trust.

Modern advertising plays on our anxieties: one's looks, the cleanliness of one's bathroom, etc.

God has been absent from the garden, but on return calls out for the man:

> They heard the sound of the LORD God walking in the garden at the time of the evening breeze, and the man and his wife hid themselves from the presence of the LORD God among the trees of the garden. But the LORD God called to the man, and said to him, 'Where are you?' He said, 'I heard the sound of thee in the garden, and I was afraid, because I was naked; and I hid myself.'
>
> *Genesis 3:8-10*

Compared with the woman's conversation with the serpent in which the plural was used by both participants, the man replies only for himself: 'I heard... I was afraid... I was naked... I hid'. Unity between the man and woman is shattered. The man does not respond to the particular question that God asked. Out of his guilt he responds to the question he thought he was being asked, 'Why are you hiding?'

God focuses on only one part of the response:

> He said, 'Who told you that you were naked? Have you eaten from the tree which I commanded you not to eat?' The man said, 'The woman whom You gave to be with me, she gave me fruit from the tree, and I ate.'
>
> *Genesis 3:11-12*

God's interest is in human obedience to the divine command 'do not eat'. In replying, the man blames both the woman and God before admitting his own disobedience. Like the older brother who distances himself from his younger sibling, by calling him 'your son', in the parable of Luke 15:30, the man separates himself from the woman 'who You gave to be with me'.

Unlike God's two questions to the man, God's question to the woman suggests that God accepted the man's account of the actions of the woman:

> Then the LORD God said to the woman, 'What is this that you have done?' The woman said, 'The serpent tricked me, and I ate."
>
> *Genesis 3:13*

Like the man, the woman shifts the blame, admitting her role only after blaming the serpent. She also answers in the singular. Blame has entered human relationships, as enacted by both the man and the woman.

The story moves to a scene of divine judgement which is presented in poetic form. The serpent is pronounced guilty without a trial and its 'slyness', *arum*, has now become 'to curse', *aror*. It will crawl on the ground and eat dust, the pre-creation element of all life:

> The LORD God said to the serpent,
> 'Because you have done this,
> cursed are you above all animals
> and above all wild creatures;
> upon your belly you shall go,
> and dust you shall eat
> all the days of your life.
> I will put enmity between you and the woman,
> and between your offspring and hers;
> he will strike your head,
> and you will strike his heel'.
>
> *Genesis 3:14-15*

The relationship between human beings and animals has changed from one of naming to one of enmity. Because the serpent spoke to the woman, the relationship between them is a particular focus. A symbol of the old belief system had tempted a woman, who had power in the goddess religion, to disobey a command of the ascendant male god. The serpent disappears from the story, but not from history.

Canby Jones emphasises the focal role of Genesis 3:15 to early Friends: 'Fox and his contemporaries saw the whole New Testament Gospel in seminal or encapsulated form in this passage'.[33] For George Fox, 'the promised Seed, which bruiseth the head of the serpent... it is he that opens the eyes of the blind. For God made men and woman perfect by Christ Jesus who comes to bruise the serpent's head', was 'the first promise of Christ'.[34]

God's statement to the woman is brief. The word 'curse' is missing and God focuses on the consequences of her disobedience:

> To the woman He said,
> 'I will greatly increase your pangs in childbearing;
> in pain you shall bring forth children,
> yet your desire shall be for your husband,
> and he shall rule over you.'
>
> *Genesis 3:16*

Childbirth will be painful, unlike that of the goddess who gave birth painlessly. Clergymen in the nineteenth century quoted Genesis 2:1 as support for the use of anaesthesia, but also used Genesis 3:16 as support for their opposition to its use during childbirth. The mother goddess and her protection in childbirth are no longer available to the woman.

The healthy sexual desire of the woman for the man, part of the harmony which was present at the end of Genesis 2, shatters. The man will rule over the woman instead of being her equal. The mutuality of sexual relations has broken down: 'Sexual attraction creates, for the moment, the illusion of union, yet without love this "union" leaves strangers as far apart as they were before - sometimes it even makes them hate each other, because when the illusion has gone they feel their estrangement even more markedly than before.'[35]

When challenged by Nathaniel Coleman about his understanding of the equality of men and women in relation to Genesis 3:16, George Fox emphasised that when one lives in the restored relationship offered by Christ, equality is the norm.[36]

Since the creation of the woman, *ish* and *ishah* have been used to show the close relationship between the two human beings. Now the narrator returns to the use of *adam,* but this is no longer the original groundling. It is Adam the man, separated from the close relationship with the woman because of disobedience. Adam's punishment begins with a reminder of the original link between the groundling and the ground:

> And to the man he said,
> 'Because you have listened to the voice of your wife,
> and have eaten of the tree of which I commanded you,
> "You shall not eat of it,"
> cursed is the ground because of you;
> in toil you shall eat of it all the days of your life;
> thorns and thistles it shall bring forth for you;
> and you shall eat the plants of the field.
> By the sweat of your face
> you shall eat bread
> until you return to the ground,
> for out of it you were taken;
> you are dust,
> and to dust you shall return.'
>
> *Genesis 3:17-19*

The man is not cursed, but the ground is cursed, as a result of which the 'tilling and keeping' of the garden becomes much more difficult. The punishment results from disobedience and is linked to eating. Instead of picking fruit, grain needs to be cultivated and turned into bread for sustenance. Work has become labour, *issabon*, a word used also in verse 16 for childbirth for the woman. Formed from the ground, Adam will return to it at death.

Although the woman is not cursed in the text, women have inherited a double curse from interpretations of these verses. One is women's association with evil. The *Malleus Malleficarum*, the fifteenth century witch-hunters' manual, states: 'In the Old Testament, the Scriptures have much to say that is evil about women, and this is because of the first temptress, Eve, and her imitators.'[37] The second is women's association with nature, 'because you have listened to the voice of your wife... cursed is the ground', represented here by its link to goddess worship. As the development of spirit was increasingly promoted, links with the body, whether associated with sexuality or with nature, were seen as hindrances to spiritual progress. The long history of the degradation of women and creation can be attributed to the excessive and distorted emphasis on obedience to Genesis 3:16-18.[38]

In God's speech to the man, there is no mention of a change in sexual awareness. But relationship is changed even when only one partner is fully aware of this. God created humankind to be workers and lovers. Sexuality and work are two of the main aspects of adult life, and unfortunately for many people both sexual relations and career take on the relationship of commodity. Self-esteem and dignity are aspects of our lives that we may have to struggle to retain. We still rely on fig leaves, though they may take different forms.

Replacing *shalom* are the cursing of the ground, alienated labour, enmity between serpent and woman, and sexuality that is not mutually understood. Now Adam can name the woman, indicating his power over her. He no longer sees her as an equal, but as the bringer of life, Eve, an important role now that they are fully aware that death is part of their experience. God makes clothes of skin that will be more durable than those of leaves. In making the clothes, God becomes the first killer of animal life:

> The man named his wife Eve, because she was the mother of all living. And the LORD God made garments of skins for the man and for his wife, and clothed them.
>
> *Genesis 3:20-1*

Chavvah, Eve, means 'mother of all living'. A Hebrew verb which uses the same consonants means 'to lie down flat on one's belly', and in many Semitic languages the noun means 'serpent'.[39] Eve is given the name of the old mother goddess, but it is a curse, not a blessing.

Having made more appropriate clothing for the couple (by sacrificing animals!) God muses about the situation:

> Then the LORD God said, 'See, the man has become like one of us, knowing good and evil; and now, he might reach out his hand and take also from the Tree of Life, and eat, and live forever.'
>
> *Genesis 3:22*

Is God addressing other gods, or using the royal 'we'? Death was the original result of eating from the tree (Genesis 2:17). God now suggests there is another potential future in which the man and woman have immortality. Was the serpent right, or is this spoken ironically? Human beings are clearly not god-like in their present state, but the Tree of

Life is still accessible to them. The sentence is incomplete, but the subsequent action completes the thought:

> ... therefore the LORD God sent him forth from the garden of Eden, to till the ground from which he was taken. He drove out the man; and at the east of the garden of Eden he placed the Cherubim, and a sword flaming and turning to guard the way to the Tree of Life.
>
> *Genesis 3:23-24*

❋　❋　❋

When the man and woman listened to and obeyed God in the garden there was an atmosphere of mutuality and equity. Now there is control and distortion. How does knowledge affect the human community? How do we define and observe appropriate boundaries?

The author may have had a topical concern in mind when writing this story, patterning the adventures of the groundling/Adam on King David's life. Both were recipients of God's gifts, both were raised to special roles, lived in special place, had important responsibilities and freedom with limits. Both enjoyed sovereignty, were attracted to 'forbidden fruit', and were aware of doing wrong. Both were judged and received new hope with new life.[40] The Israelites may have been wondering what they had got themselves into with their new-fangled monarchy.

Knowledge leads to freedom to act and offers the potential of control. In a new kingdom the rulers had to learn their boundaries. David had knowledge about Uriah and used this to 'know' Bathsheba. Solomon sought wisdom. Unfortunately, instead of inheriting his father's gifts, Rehoboam inherited his grandfather's foolishness and lust for life.

❋　❋　❋

At the end of the story Adam returns to where the groundling began life, outside the garden. He continues the original role of the groundling, tilling the ground. *Shalom* has been lost. God prevents any return to the garden and thus access to eternal life[41] by placing armed cherubim as guardians. The groundling was 'to keep', *shmr*, the earth, now the cherubim, 'keep/guard', *shmr*, the garden, while Adam tills the cursed ground.

Early Friends interpreted the events in the garden as a fall from obedience to God into the power of Satan, the god of the world. They did not accept that men and women were still under the power of the fall, since they experienced Christ's coming as a restoration to 'nature in its course',[42] the original state of man and woman in the garden.

> Now I was come in spirit through the flaming sword into the paradise of God. All things were new, and all the creation gave another smell unto me that before, beyond what words can utter. I knew nothing but pureness and innocency, and righteousness, being renewed up into the image of God by Christ Jesus, so that I say I was come up into the state of Adam which he was in before he fell.' This opening of George Fox included 'a more steadfast state than Adam's in innocency, even into a state of Jesus Christ, that should never fall'.[43]

Paradise lost. Traditional interpretations of this story have focused on a fall that permeates most of Christianity, and Friends are still affected by this dominant interpretation despite the life-changing insights of George Fox.

Although there are portrayals of God in the scriptures which continue the sense of punishment, there are also other indications of the continuance of God's original purpose for men and women. The Song of Solomon, often allegorized as the relationship between God and Israel or between Christ and the church, is an erotic love story in which the partners enjoy the original relationship experienced by the man and woman in the garden. The woman as keeper of the vineyard invites her lover to join her there, in a poem in which the vineyard stands for erotic pleasure and lovemaking:

> Let us go out early to the vineyards,
> and see whether the vines have budded,
> whether the grape blossoms have opened
> and the pomegranates are in bloom.
> There I will give you my love.
>
> *Song of Solomon 7:12*

Sexual love is unequivocally good and brings *shalom*, 'then I was in his eyes as one who brings peace' (Song of Solomon 8:10). Other references to work in creation which is linked with pleasure are Isaiah 5:1, 27:2, Jeremiah 31:5 and Micah 4:4. These suggest that mutually healthy relationships with other human beings and with the earth can be restored through work.

Unfortunately the New Testament record and subsequent interpretations on this aspect of *shalom* are not helpful. Jesus's unique birth and the absence of any mention of his sexuality in the canonical gospels have led to a Christianity which often sees sexual intimacy as a poor second choice to celibacy. However, the gospel record of Jesus' relationships with women portrays a sense of acceptance of women that is very different from the expectations of his culture. On one of his better days, Paul affirms the equality of women and men, 'There is no longer Jew or Greek, there is no longer slave or free, there is no longer male and female, for all of you are one in Christ Jesus' (Galatians 3:28). However, in struggling with the daily realities of human relations, Paul turns to Genesis 3 as its cause, 'Therefore, just as sin came into the world though one man, and death came through sin, and so sin spread, because all have sinned', in Romans 5:12.

What may be have been equally destructive is the pushing of any restoration into an apocalyptic future:

> For the creation waits with eager longing for the revealing of the children of God; for the creation was subjected to futility, not of its own will but by the will of the one who subjected it, in hope that the creation itself will be set free from its bondage to decay and will obtain the freedom of the glory of the children of God.
>
> *Romans 8:19-21*

This was strongly challenged by early Friends, who found biblical confirmation in Paul: 'So if anyone is in Christ there is a new creation, everything old has passed away; see everything has become new!' (2 Corinthians 5:17).

Despite this experience of Paul and of early Friends, we have inherited the other Pauline scenario of 'the Fall'.

Chapter IV

MURDER AND MORE: GENESIS 4-11

THE harmony of creation has been shattered, but there is still more to come. Like others of these early stories, the story of Cain and Abel is well-known but familiarity may prevent us from seeing the nuances in the text.

> Now the man knew Eve his wife, and she conceived and bore Cain, saying, 'I have produced a man with the help of the LORD.' Next she bore his brother Abel. Now Abel was a keeper of sheep, and Cain a tiller of the ground.
> *Genesis 4:1-2*

Eve conceives and bears a son, Cain. Cain is *qaneh*, 'shaft' in Hebrew, and is punned with *qanah*, 'I have produced.' This is the first creation not handled directly by God. The woman takes on both divine and earthy roles in conceiving, containing, birthing and nurturing life. Here then, is an opportunity for new life. A second son, Abel, *habel*, 'breath' or 'wind', which also implies 'emptiness',[1] is also born.

The sons have different livelihoods as nomadic herdsman and agriculturist, with Cain sharing Adam's work. The Bronze Age conflict between the nomadic Semitic tribes from the Syro-Arabian desert and the sedentary farmers of the river valleys are reflected in this story. Behind Cain and Abel lies the Hebrew conquest of Canaan during which time Hebrew shepherds clashed with Canaanite farmers.

The nomadic existence was an older style of life than settled agricultural life. Abel the younger son, takes on the older role, reflecting the tendency in Genesis for a younger son to be favoured. For example, Isaac is favoured over Ishmael, Jacob over Esau, and Joseph over his brothers.

Like the other stories we have examined, there are Near Eastern parallels to this account of Cain and Abel. In a Sumerian story, Inanna is urged to marry a shepherd, but prefers a farmer. In a boasting match, Dumuzi, the shepherd, claims that his animals are better than Enkimdu's produce, picking a quarrel with him. Enkimdu responds by inviting Dumuzi to graze his flock anywhere on his land. Inanna marries Dumuzi and Enkimdu attends their wedding - a rare, happy outcome.[2]

> In the course of time Cain brought to the LORD an offering of the fruit of the ground, and Abel for his part brought of the firstlings of his flock, their fat portions. And the LORD had regard for Abel and his offering, but for Cain and his offering he had no regard. So Cain was very angry, and his countenance fell.
>
> *Genesis 4:3-5*

This story incorporates aspects of the widely accepted system of sacrifices in the ancient Near East.[3] Most nations recognised their dependence on divine power, and sought to maintain the goodwill of the gods by thanking them for their provision of food and children. The offering of the first fruits showed both a sense of gratitude and a sense of fear, that the gods might turn their backs if humankind forgot its dependence on them. There was also an element of trust: if the first crop was given, more would be produced.

Cain's offering is modified in the Hebrew by the word 'some', 'some of the fruits of the earth', compared with the best of Abel's flock. This lack of respect by Cain may not be the original focus of the author. Why does God seems to reject some offerings and accept others? Cain's anger may be in response to the frustration of not knowing the reason for his rejection. In the Genesis narrative God disrupts, tantalizes, creates tension and reveals the dark side of life.

In his anger, Cain's face fell:

> The LORD said to Cain, 'Why are you angry, and why has your countenance fallen? If you do well, will you not be accepted? And if you do not do well, sin is lurking at the door; its desire is for you, but you must master it.'
>
> *Genesis 4:6-7*

The NRSV translation misses the word play on the opposite of 'fall': 'will you not be accepted,' is literally 'there is a lifting up.' The fallen face can be lifted up if Cain does well, giving his best. God warns Cain, and tries to encourage him to engage in self-examination and reflect on his anger.

Verse 7 has been said to be the most difficult verse in Genesis. It is probably a late addition to the text, but as it stands it emphasises that Cain knew he was fully responsible for his actions.

In Genesis 1:28 the man and woman are given dominion; in Genesis 3:16 the man rules the woman; now Cain is given the choice, to rule over sin or to let sin rule him. In *East of Eden*, John Steinbeck plays with the Hebrew word *timshel*, 'you shall rule/master', exploring its ambiguity. Is it an invitation, a challenge or a promise?[4]

Sin is introduced into the biblical text. The verb *chata* means 'missing' or 'not reaching a target', and is often used when God's law is violated. This text presents sin as a wild animal or demon always ready to attack and cause the intended aim to go astray.

In his anger and depression Cain is a ready victim of this destructive force. Like the groundling who was given a choice of food, Cain too is given a choice.

Cain said to his brother Abel, 'Let us go out to the field'. And when they were in the field, Cain rose up against his brother Abel, and killed him.

Genesis 4:8

Cain and God enter into a conversation that echoes the discussion between the man and God in the garden, and like the man, Cain takes the defensive:

Then the LORD said to Cain, 'Where is Abel your brother?' He said, 'I do not know; am I my brother's keeper?' And the LORD said, 'What have you done? Listen, your brother's blood is crying out to me from the ground! And now you are cursed from the ground, which has opened its mouth to receive your brother's blood from your hand. When you till the ground, it shall no longer yield to you its strength; you will be a fugitive and a wanderer on the earth.'

Genesis 4:9-11

When God called to the man he avoided a direct answer and gave his own interpretation of events, but did eventually admit to eating the fruit. Cain lies about murdering Abel and asks God a question. Should we act as our brothers' keepers? Fraternal responsibility is a theme of much of Genesis in chapters 37-50. Family relationships are difficult as even Romulus and Remus knew. We cannot hover over our siblings, but neither can we reject them.

Verse 10 is the dramatic focal point of the story. The harmony of creation is further reduced. The voice of the blood, *dam*, of your brother, *ach*, cries from the ground, *adamah*. The ground, cursed in Genesis 3:17, now accuses and curses Cain. Later in the biblical text God sends human mediators to accuse those who have murdered: Nathan accuses David, (2 Samuel 12) and Elijah reveals Ahab's sin (1 Kings 21).

Cain is the first human being to be cursed. God tells Cain he will no longer get his sustenance from the ground. Because he is banished, he will not be able to rely on family for nourishment, security or support, and so becomes the first prodigal son. Adam was banned from the garden and had to work the soil. Now Cain is banned from the soil. To nomads banishment was death.

> Cain said to the LORD, 'My punishment is greater than I can bear! Today you have driven me away from the soil, and I shall be hidden from your face; and I shall be a fugitive and a wanderer on the earth, and anyone who meets me may kill me'. Then the LORD said to him, 'Not so! Whoever kills Cain will suffer a sevenfold vengeance.' And the LORD put a mark on Cain, so that no one who came upon him would kill him. Then Cain went away from the presence of the LORD, and settled in the land of Nod, east of Eden.
>
> *Genesis 4:12-16*

God's punishment is moderated after Cain's fearful pleading. The mark he receives is one of protection, but shows both guilt and grace. God's threat to other human beings was that none of them should execute God's decision. Banishment with all its consequences was the punishment, not death. Cain settles in *Nod*, Hebrew for 'wandering', a place of alienation from God. In later biblical interpretations of this story, Cain is identified as the son of Satan (1 John 3:12), or with the serpent (4 Maccabees 18:8).

For George Fox, the story of Cain along with those of 'other wicked men of former times', becomes a challenge to readers of the Bible:

> And I saw the state of those, both priests and people, who in reading the scriptures, cry out much against Cain,

Esau and Judas, and other wicked men of former times, mentioned in the holy scriptures; but do not see the nature of Cain, of Esau, of Judas, and those others in themselves. And they said it was they, they, they that were the bad people; putting it off from themselves: but when some of these came, with the light and spirit of Truth, to see into themselves, then they came to say, 'I, I, I, it is I myself that have been the Ishmael and the Esau.'[5]

Although some people identify their own weaknesses in these biblical characters, others who deny any link will continue to live in a state of first birth by refusing to heed the Inward Teacher, 'Cain was the first birth... now tell Cain the envious murderer of a silent meeting or waiting upon God, when he is a vagabond from that of God within him...'[6] Cain is also seen as an example of priests who 'turned against the righteous', who will not longer be able to 'ride' the people.[7] Cain will not have eternal life or dominion, 'but be in fears and get into cities'.[8]

Madeleine L'Engle brings a particularly female interpretation to the story:

There had never been children before.

Eve did not know what was happening to her, with her belly swelling and movement within it and then a great ripping and tearing. There was terror and there was pain. And then Cain, squally, red-faced and angry at the indignity of birth. The first child. He would have preferred simply to have been formed of dust.

When Abel was conceived Eve understood what was happening, so perhaps it was easier to hold Abel, to gentle him against her breast, knowing that the hungry lips were searching only for milk, not trying to bite or hurt and destroy.

The two children romped like lion cubs. They vied for love. They loved and hated and were jealous. But it was all easier for Abel.
So Cain hit him. There had never before been death. He did not know why Abel did not get up and hit him back. He did not know that he had brought death into the world, and that he would bear its mark, so would we.[9]

This is more than a story of sibling rivalry. It addresses the fear of human beings who know they have done wrong. It opens the question of our experience of God whom we may not always experience as a God of love. But it does confirm that God will not totally let go of us.

❋ ❋ ❋

Cain bears offspring. The biblical text is not distracted by the question of where he found a spouse. Instead it inexorably follows the fate of its main characters. Lamech is born in the fifth generation after Cain. Each of Lamech's sons have roles that are part of the lives of semi-nomads: they become the ancestors of all who have tents and cattle, metal workers and musicians who were the historians of the tribe.

Lamech boasts to his wives that he kills those who wound him and even kills young boys who touch him:

> I have slain a man for wounding me,
> a young man for striking me.
> If Cain is avenged sevenfold,
> truly Lamech seventy-sevenfold.

Genesis 4:23-24

This is an example of a taunt song, an old form of poetry, which is still found in school playgrounds. In nomadic culture any breach of honour is responded to by violence. Even so, Lamech's vengeance is extreme. If God's revenge for killing Cain was to have been sevenfold, then if he, Lamech is killed, the revenge should be seventy-sevenfold. In the Hebrew Bible seven denotes completeness, and so Lamech is portrayed as totally inhuman. The first human murderer did so in the heat of anger. Now Lamech is now prepared to glorify revenge, quoting God as his justification. Jesus's injunction to forgive seventy times seven, Matthew 18:22, is the absolute converse of the law of retaliation.

Some hope is expressed at the end of the chapter. Enoch is born, and people look to God for help. The earlier characters, Adam, Eve, Cain and Lamech seem to have accepted God's presence as a birth right, but have not sought God. Now there is a 'convinced' generation.

The genealogy of Adam through Seth follows, and the image of God is still part of humankind: 'he became the father of a son in his own likeness, after his image', (Genesis 5:3). Like God, but one step removed. Enoch 'walked with God' (Genesis 5:22-23). Because there is no clear indication of his death, Enoch became a focal point in the apocalyptic tradition, serving as a time-travelling guide to future events.

Each of these individuals lives a long life. By counting these and other dates, Bishop Ussher calculated that the world was created at twelve o'clock on Sunday, October 23, 4004 BCE. This was later contested, the correct date of creation being Monday, October 26, twenty one years later![10]

Before we skip over it, we need to identify a third account of creation in the text of Genesis:

> When God created humankind, he made them in the likeness of God. Male and female created he them, and he blessed them and named them 'Humankind' when they were created.
>
> *Genesis 5:1b-2*

Would we be in better shape if this was the only account of creation we had inherited? Both earlier accounts find resolution in this summary - men and women are equal and are made in God's image.

❊ ❊ ❊

Noah is born in the tenth generation after Adam, and the tenth generation before Abraham.[11] The flood therefore becomes the centre of human history before the choice of a particular nation by God.

Noah's father predicts that Noah will reverse the curse of the ground that occurred in Genesis 3:17:

> Out of the ground which the LORD has cursed this one shall bring us relief from our work and from the toil of our hands.
>
> *Genesis 5:29*

Before the Noah story proceeds, a strange interlude intervenes:

> When people began to multiply on the face of the ground, and daughters were born to them, the sons of God saw that they were fair; and they took wives for themselves of all that they chose. Then the LORD said, 'My spirit shall not abide in mortals forever for they are flesh; their days shall be one hundred and twenty years.' The *Nephilim* were on the earth in those days - and also afterward - when the sons of God went into the daughters of humans, who bore children to them. These were the heroes that were of old, the warriors of renown.
>
> *Genesis 6:1-4*

The sons of God are members of God's heavenly assembly. They praise God (Job 38:7, Psalms 29:1), and they represent foreign nations in the assembly (Deuteronomy 32:8). The term is common in other ancient Near East mythology where it refers to the pantheon of minor deities. Beginning in the seventh and sixth centuries BCE, the prophetic writers rejected the notion that other beings lived in heaven, seeing them as a foreign intrusion in Israelite monotheism. *Nephilim* also occur in Numbers 13:33 where they are the giant aboriginal inhabitants of Canaan. Joshua 12:4 speaks of Og's bedstead, an equally puzzling reference. Megalithic monuments, found by the Hebrews on their arrival in Canaan, may have encouraged legends about giants. Canaanites had the reputation of sexual immorality; their temple prostitutes made themselves available for relieving the sexual needs of the gods.[12]

God's initial response to the mating with human women is to limit human life span to one hundred and twenty years, denying again the possibility of immortality. In Genesis 3 fruit was the attractant, now sexual intercourse is the way in which the border between the realms of God and humanity is breached. Three aspects of relationship and the difficulties in maintaining this have now been examined: between men and woman, between siblings and between the human and divine or those with different power. At Babel, community will challenge God.

If J was writing from the perspective of the Jerusalem court, there may be a criticism of the behaviour of the king(s) embedded in this story. The Israelites struggled over the question of having a monarchy, feeling that God was their king, and that human kings would abuse their power. Taking beautiful women was one such temptation. The full meaning of the story in context is not clear, other than to reinforce the spread of evil in creation.

New Testament writers interpret this story as a dangerous

disordering of creation (2 Peter 2:4, Jude 6). An alternative interpretation is to see this as a caution to all elements of creation who break the boundaries set by God.

'A warning to hypocrite Quakers who go to the world for a wife' uses the story of the sons of God marrying daughters of men as the reason why Friends should marry within the group and avoid ceremonies conducted by priests.[13]

❊   ❊   ❊

There are flood stories found in the myths and legends of cultures from around the world, with the flood being the archetype of human catastrophe. Floods were common in the Tigris and Euphrates valley and were very destructive. As civilisations developed, large irrigation schemes were constructed and floods frequently destroyed these and the means of livelihood of the farmers. The Sumerians had five cities wiped out by such a flood.

The earliest flood story found in the Near East is Sumerian from about 3000 BCE. The partial tablets describe how the gods are angered because human beings keep them awake by the noise they make at night. The gods decide to destroy humankind with a flood, but two gods regret the decision and choose Ziusudra whom they instruct to build a boat. Ziusudra is saved. He makes sacrifices to Utu the sun and is elevated to godhood.[14]

The *Epic of Gilgamesh* from Babylon also has a long and very detailed flood sequence. Utnapishtim tells Gilgamesh his story. The gods felt that human beings were becoming too self-sufficient, yet some gods wanted to save humankind. Utnapishtim heard the gods' voices through the reed wall of his home, telling him to build a large ship and to place in it the seed of all living things. Plans were given in great detail. The huge structure was built and stockpiled within seven days. Besides the animals and Utnapishtim's family, craftsmen also entered the ship. The terrible storm lasted six days and nights after which a flood covered the land, leaving only mountain tops visible. All life was destroyed and even the gods had to scramble to safety. A dove, a swallow and a raven were released, and an offering was made to the gods who crowded round the altar like flies.[15]

Missing from the Noah story are the goddesses of earlier versions of the flood story. In both Sumerian and Babylonian stories, the goddesses lament the destruction of the people they had brought into being. In the Babylonian story, Ishtar placed her necklace in the sky and swore to remember the time of destruction. The birds of the Genesis account, the raven and the dove, were sacred to Ishtar.

The story of Noah is clearly linked to these myths and it is interesting to see how it has been edited to reflect a belief in a monotheistic god and mortal human beings. The Noah story as we have received it is a combination of two Israelite versions, one by J and the other by P (see Appendix). Each author has a particular perspective and these need to be accepted as such and not thought as internal contradictions. Instead of being the audience for a play in which the story unfolds in a logical sequence, we are watching an experimental video with its different camera perspectives, close ups and repetitions.

By this time God has had enough:

> The LORD saw that the wickedness of humankind was great in the earth, and that every inclination of the thoughts of their hearts was only evil continually. And the LORD was sorry that he had made humankind on the earth, and it grieved him to his heart. So the LORD said, 'I will blot out from the earth the human beings I have created - people together with animals and creeping

things and birds of the air, for I am sorry that I have made them.'

Genesis 6:5-7

The 'very good' of Genesis 1 has become 'I will blot it out'. As in the earlier stories, God's mind can be changed. Noah was a righteous man, father of three sons, and 'found favour in the eyes of the LORD' (Genesis 6:8). Noah is to become the new Adam.

Unlike the other ancient Near Eastern flood stories, where the gods take revenge on humankind for petty reasons, this flood is presented as the result of human evil. Divine justice is at stake. For a people who had experienced floods this was the only rationale they could give. God does not destroy creation with a sense of joy or sadistic pleasure:

> And the LORD was sorry that he had made man on the earth, and it grieved him to his heart.
>
> *Genesis 6:6*

God instructs Noah to build an ark. The ark is about 450 feet long, 75 feet wide and 45 feet high. It is immense. The only other biblical use of the Hebrew word *teba*, 'ark' is in Exodus 2:3-5, where it is the basket that saves Moses from drowning.

> But I will establish my covenant with you; and you shall come into the ark, you, your sons, your wife, and your sons' wives with you. And of every living thing of all flesh, you shall bring two of every sort into the ark, to keep them alive with you; they shall be male and female. Of the birds according to their kinds, and of the animals according to their kinds, of every creeping thing of the ground according to its kind, two of every sort shall come in to you, to keep them alive. Also take with you every sort of food that is eaten, and store it up; and it shall serve as food for you and for them.
>
> *Genesis 6:18-21*

God makes a covenant with Noah, but this is not as complex as the covenants of later times. Here it is a promise by God to save the variety of creation. Later covenants involved commitments by both parties. Here Noah's role is to be obedient to God's instructions (Genesis 6:22).

God's order to gather one pair of all animal species comes from the Priestly writer. For this writer, sacrifice did not begin until after the law had been given to Moses. As we reach J's account, seven pairs of clean animals are needed to prepare for the sacrifice and leave sufficient to breed (Genesis 7:2-3).

Before anything else happens there is a seven day wait, paralleling the time of the first creation, Genesis 7:10. Now creation is reversed:

> ... on that day all the fountains of the great deep burst forth, and the windows of the heavens were opened. And rain fell upon the earth forty days and forty nights.
>
> *Genesis 7:11-12*

Creation in Genesis 1 was the result of God's controlling the waters. Now God lets go. The flood, *mabul* in Hebrew, is the water above the dome in Genesis 1:7. The dome collapses and chaos reigns, all except for the ark (Genesis 7:17-24). The duration of the flood is sufficient to blot out every living thing.

Creation occurs again as God remembers Noah:

> And God made a wind blow over the earth, and the waters subsided; the fountains of the deep and the windows of the heavens were closed, the rain from the heavens was restrained, and the waters receded from the earth continually.
>
> *Genesis 8:1b-3a*

The 'wind from God swept over the face of the waters' again as in Genesis 1:2. Eventually the ark comes to rest on the mountains of Ararat. Ararat in Armenia is 5165 metres high (16,945 feet), the highest mountain in the Near East. Claims are still made in tabloid magazines about the discovery of huge structures stranded high on the mountain.

It takes a long time for the flood waters to recede, Genesis 8:3-6. A raven is sent out and does not return. Ravens are the bird of choice in the Babylonian story. Noah sends out a dove that returns because there is no dry ground. After seven days it is released again and returns with a live branch, indicating that dry ground has emerged. After another seven day wait the dove is released and does not return. Pliny later tells of ships having birds that were released to fly towards land, so that the sailors could set a course to follow.[16]

On God's command, Noah leaves the ark. He and the creatures are given the same instructions as in Genesis 1:22 and 28, 'be fruitful and multiply', Genesis 8:17. Is Noah the new creation? Has sin been washed away?

Noah builds an altar and offers sacrifices to God, the odour of which pleases God (Genesis 8:20). God reflects alone:

> I will never again curse the ground because of humankind, for the inclination of the human heart is evil from youth; nor will I ever again destroy every living creature as I have done.
> As long as the earth endures,
> seedtime and harvest, cold and heat,
> summer and winter, day and night,
> shall not cease.

> *Genesis 8:21b-22*

In this new creation humankind are unchanged from Genesis 6:5. What changes has the flood effected? God, or the story's perception of God, has changed. There will no longer be destruction by God because of human weakness. Instead of God 'uncreating' as punishment, God will sustain an ordered world. The new relationship will be between a grieved God and a resistant world. There is a promise of regular seasons which will not need to be coerced from the gods through sacrifice and annual reenactment. The command to be fruitful and fill the earth is restated, but this still is not Eden. The relationship between humankind and animals is characterized by 'dread and fear' (Genesis 9:2). Humans may now eat meat (Genesis 9:3), but there is a limitation. Blood signified life, so this had to be removed before the flesh of the animal could be eaten. The act of killing animals for food takes on a sacramental awareness, very different from the pre-flood culture of senseless violence.[17]

Capital punishment is a reality (Genesis 9:6). Murder is an attack on God's right of dominion over all creation, so anyone who oversteps this boundary will be punished. God's generosity to Cain is forgotten. Instead of the ground being cursed, the human who kills will be held accountable. The relationships between victim, murderer, community and the land are now maintained by an intricate system of checks and balances,[18] which is fully detailed in Leviticus.

God is ready to make a covenant in which there is no expectation in return from the human beings:

> 'As for me, I am establishing my covenant with you and your descendants after you, and with every living creature that is with you, the birds, the domestic animals, and every animal of the earth with you, as many as came out of the ark. I establish my covenant with you, that never again shall all flesh be cut off by the waters of a flood, and never again shall there be a flood to destroy the earth.'

And God said, 'This is the sign of the covenant that I make between me and you and every living creature that is with you, for all future generations: I set my bow in the clouds, and it shall be a sign of the covenant between me and the earth. When I bring clouds over the earth and the bow is seen in the clouds, I will remember my covenant which is between me and you and every living creature of all flesh; and the waters shall never again become a flood to destroy all flesh.'

Genesis 9:9-15

The rainbow is a reminder to both God and humankind of the promise that the earth will not be destroyed by God. There is still evil, but it is not rooted in God's anger. The rainbow may symbolise an undrawn bow showing that God is no longer seeking victory over chaos, or over his tendency to punish. The first creation ended with Sabbath rest, this creation ends with God resting his bow.[19]

Interpersonal relationships in this re-creation are seen as part of the divine order, and their breakdown threatens creation itself:

There is no faithfulness or loyalty, and no knowledge of God in the land.
Swearing, lying, and murder, and stealing and adultery break out;
bloodshed follows bloodshed.
Therefore the land mourns, and all who live in it languish:
together with the wild animals and the birds of the air, even the fish of the sea are perishing.

Hosea 4:1b-3

The author recognises that although God has rejected destructive violence and control over creation, humankind, continuing in its pre-flood characteristics, is not able to maintain creation nonviolently.

Life can continue after the flood. Noah plants a vineyard, caring for the earth. The Hebrew scriptures are not preoccupied with the abuse of alcohol, and it is usually seen as a gift to be used in the celebration of creation. Humankind has to discern the knife edge in this situation, as in many others. Grapes are good but may also be dangerous.

Noah was the first tiller of the soil. He planted a vineyard:

> ... and he drank of the wine, and became drunk, and lay uncovered in his tent. And Ham, the father of Canaan, saw the nakedness of his father, and told his two brothers outside. Then Shem and Japheth took a garment, laid it upon both their shoulders, and walked backward and covered the nakedness of their father; their faces were turned away, and they did not see their father's nakedness. When Noah awoke from his wine and knew what his youngest son had done to him, he said, 'Cursed be Canaan; a slave of slaves shall he be to his brothers.' He also said, 'Blessed by the LORD my God be Shem; and let Canaan be his slave.'
>
> *Genesis 9:21-27*

Nakedness was shameful in Judaism, representing a loss of human dignity. The shame of nakedness fell on the observer, not on the naked person. The observer was expected to cover the nakedness and not speak about it, Leviticus 18. Ham saw his father naked and his responsibility was to cover him up, protecting the authority of the head of the family. As punishment his heirs became slaves, an unnatural situation that is not natural within families. Some interpreters see a sexual reference here. Again the son was not to dishonour the parent by speaking of the event. The story leaves us with questions about its full meaning, but clearly is used here to justify the later struggles between Israel and Canaan.

As part of the law relating to payment of debt, any garments taken as payment had to be returned at night (Exodus 22:25-7, Amos 2:7-8). Outer garments were used as blankets by the poor. Prophets did not only speak out against injustice, but often acted in symbolic ways that illustrated the injustice. Isaiah walked naked and barefoot as a prophetic sign for three years (Isaiah 20:1-6).

Jesus took the tradition against nakedness to its extreme as he challenged the injustice of his times, '... and if anyone wants to sue you and take your coat, give your cloak as well' (Matthew 5:40), paralleled in Luke by '... and from anyone who takes away your coat do not withhold even your shirt' (Luke 6:29). There was a high level of debt in first century Palestine, caused by heavy Roman taxes and interest levels. Large areas of land were owned by absentee landlords, managed by stewards and worked by slaves and day labourers. The first act of the Jewish War of 66 CE was to burn the Temple treasury, where the record of debts was kept.

The members of Jesus' audience were the victims of this system. Jesus was encouraging them to transform the situation of being taken to court with no possibility of paying in a non-violent way. To strip off one's last garment, and leave it with the wealthy creditor, turns the tables. It reveals the injustice within the system, and challenges the creditor and the court to offer restoration, not punishment.[20]

The listing of the nations descended from Noah is arranged on political lines in Genesis 10. Israel is missing as it has not yet had its foundation in Abraham. All nations develop from the live-giving power of God:

> From one ancestor he made all nations to inhabit the whole earth... so that they would search for God and perhaps grope for him and find him--though indeed he

is not far from each one of us. For 'In him we have life and move and have our being.'

Acts 17:26-28

The tower of Babel, the last story in this part of Genesis, is also well-known. There are tower stories in many traditions. In Africa there is usually destruction rather than dispersion or confusion. The Sumerian story revolves round the rivalry between the gods, during which the god of wisdom changed human speech to cause confusion.[21] In the *Enuma Elish* it takes a year to prepare sacred bricks.

When the Greek historian Herodotus visited Babylon about 450 BCE, he saw the Tower of Babel. The great ziggurat was still used as a temple. At its summit stood a shrine built of blue-glazed brick with a couch and a golden table. Here Marduk spent each new year's night in the company of local maidens.[22]

The sophisticated structure built into the narrative of Genesis 11:1-9 is diagrammed below. The numbers indicate verses 1-8, and the indentations show the parallel structure built into the story, peaking at verse 5 and then reversing:

the *whole earth* had *one language* 1
    settled there 2
        one another 3
            come *let us make bricks*
              let us *build* 4
                  a *city* and a *tower*
                      the LORD came down 5
                  the *city* and the *tower*
              mortals had *built*
            come *let us ... confuse* 7
        one another's speech
    scattered abroad from there 8
confused the language of *all the earth* 9

The original context of the story was a polemic against Babylon. Israelites did not make bricks or use bitumen for building. Their own land had lots of stone, and mortar was used in construction. Like the man and the woman who covered their nakedness with fig leaves, these builders chose a strange material for their creation. Their goals are listed in an egocentric statement:

> 'Come let us build ourselves a city, and a tower with its top in the heavens, and let us make a name for ourselves...'
>
> *Genesis 11:4a*

The tower is not as impressive as they may think, for God has to leave heaven and come down to earth before it can be seen!

For George Fox the languages of Babel are in contrast to the Word of God that leads people out of confusion and evil into a community of faith.[23] He also questions the academic focus on biblical languages,[24] and Margaret Fell accuses priests of 'building Babel in the many languages which God is coming to confound'.[25]

The nations had originally been spread over the earth. At Babel they have come together and seek to enter heaven. God scatters them again. 'Confuse their language' is *balal* in Hebrew, a pun on *babel*, which means 'door of God'. The door is soundly closed. Verse 7, 'will not understand one another's speech', *shema*, may also be translated as 'they do not listen to one another', reflecting the ongoing challenge for human beings to listen and discern. In Genesis 1 God spoke creation into existence. In Genesis 3 the man and woman did not listen to God's instructions to them. Not listening is a frequent element of prophetic challenge, Jeremiah 5:21, 7:13, 11:10.

The nations were scattered and would not gather again or be able to communicate until:

> All of them were filled with the Holy Spirit and began to speak in other languages, as the Spirit gave them ability. And there were devout Jews from every nation living in Jerusalem. And at this sound the crowd gathered and was bewildered because each one heard them speaking in the native language of each... All were amazed and perplexed and said one to another, 'What does this mean?'
>
> *Acts 2: 2-12*

Pentecost offers a new opportunity to listen and so a new era can begin.

Chapter V

THE VOYAGE CONTINUES[1]

IN 1983 the World Council of Churches established a conciliar process of mutual commitment to justice, peace and the integrity of creation. Its goals were to speak and act together, to respond out of faith experience, to recognise the biblical basis for the work and to respect, consult and incorporate resources from other faith traditions.[2] 'Justice, peace and the integrity of creation' is a modern restatement of Micah's advice '... to do justice, to love kindness, and to walk humbly with your God'.[3]

The primeval history of Genesis 1-11 also voices these concerns. Can these stories with their own challenges and their clutter of later interpretations, guide us today? Is there baggage we need to leave behind? Are there new stories we need to help us as we journey?

We are all in a canoe being propelled in one direction. Some travellers look backward and try to hold on to past beliefs and behaviours. A few are arguing about long-standing differences. There are others in the middle, pretending nothing is happening. Some hide in the depths of the ship, like Jonah before he found temporary accommodation in the belly of a fish, only to have this also snatched away. Others look forward, straining to see the future, eager to learn from the changing horizon.

The change from a backward-looking perspective to one that is open to new horizons does not occur through doctrinal argument or moral appeal. Change happens when new models are offered that invite the traveller to challenge the old story and discover new energy which transforms the story or propels the searcher to look for a new vehicle.

27. *Live adventurously. When choices arise, do you take the way that offers the fullest opportunity for the use of your gifts in the service of God and the community?   Let your life speak.   When decisions have to be made, are you ready to join with others in seeking clearness, asking for God's guidance and offering counsel to one another?*

36. *Do you uphold those who are acting under concern, even if their way is not yours? Can you lay aside your own wishes and prejudices while seeking with others to find God's will for them?*

✻　✻　✻

When we approach a text, we do not encounter it alone. We also meet the layers of interpretation that accompany it. Some of this baggage is not part of the original horizon of the text, but we cannot sort this out into piles of neatly labelled luggage. We may be fortunate and lose some during our travels.

Doing justice, loving kindness and walking humbly all refer to relationship. This relationship is with God, with other human beings and with the whole of creation.

Genesis 1-11 explores these relationships through historicised fiction, offering more than one point of view on some concerns. From Genesis 1 we inherit the interpretation of a transcendent God who is separate from creation, and dualism which leads to domination and the devaluation of creation. Genesis 2-3 leaves us with 'the Fall', a dualism focused on sexuality, a God whose actions leave us with questions, and the alienation of humankind from work. Genesis 4 presents the ongoing dilemma of senseless violence and poses questions about appropriate justice. Genesis 7-10 makes us again question God's intent for the whole of creation. Genesis 11 points out the lack of trust and communication in the world. Genesis 1-11 does not seek to present final answers. Its incompleteness expresses the difficulties faced two to three thousand years ago, difficulties with which we still identify.

The theme of separation and differentiation in Genesis 1 has led to distortions in its interpretation which emphasise a separateness between God, creation and humanity. This results in a transcendent God, a godless Earth and human beings who have dominion over creation. In contrasting Israel's experience of God with those of Babylon and Canaan, the priestly writer emphasised the transcendence of God in comparison to the pantheism and polytheism of Israel's neighbours. The god of Genesis 1 is majestic, just and equitable, very different from the gods who inhabited the Earth and used human beings as slaves to respond to divine whim. In context, Genesis 1 does not rank one part of creation against another. It encourages a sense of balance and completeness. Creation, while not God, is still of God and in God.

Genesis 2 reflects a relationship with God which was both close yet treated human beings as puppets to be manipulated. Later, more 'sophisticated' biblical writers were uncomfortable with this portrait of an anthropomorphic God, an experimental potter and tailor, who was wilful, absolute and autocratic. J's directness in describing a god whose motives are not transparent to human beings was later masked by the picture of an all-mighty, all-powerful ruler. The personal involvement and communication between God and creation progressed from evening meetings in the garden to contacts through angelic messengers and occasional communication with the prophets.

We see from both P and J how an author's signature can affect a text. The priestly writer was seeking to express an experience of God which counter-balanced the influences of the Babylonian culture. This does not mean P was not inspired in his work. Genesis 1 is a majestic account of creation, and, despite the distortions of later readings it still stands as a classic text of creation. J was writing a history of her people which integrated into the old stories a sense of the challenges of the new monarchy. This was probably not intended to be a religious text. What J does present are the dilemmas individuals face in their lives, clothed by the stories of archetypal ancestors. For J, God was a mysterious force who balanced creativity with petulance, autocracy and an ability to change 'his' mind.

These stories still have power. Some would define this as a negative power which has encouraged the distortion of relationships between sexes and between humankind and creation. I see the power as being the energy released when these stories are discussed, energy which can be used in a positive way to move us forward as we seek to establish right relationships.

Christianity adds another layer of interpretation to Genesis 1-11. Jesus of Nazareth sought to establish an inclusive community which was in direct communication with God. The experience of Jesus at his baptism is recorded in creation-inspired language. The Spirit, like a dove, descended on him as he rose from the water.[4] In Jesus, the barriers between God and humanity are broken down and a direct relationship is again possible. In Christian theological terms, immanence is expressed through incarnation.

Even his closest disciples misunderstood Jesus's ministry. We are fortunate to have the various gospels that, like sketches, photos and paintings of the same person, give rich but enigmatic glimpses of the effect of this man on those whose lives he touched. It is clear that the disciples had a life-changing experience after his death. They turned from frightened individuals who deserted him,[5] into fearless witnesses of his work, as recorded in the book of Acts.

Christianity, as espoused by Paul and the early church, seemed to institutionalise this new infusion of spirit in the world. Later generations continued imposing a patriarchal straightjacket on what had been a powerful movement which engaged people directly, not through layers of bureaucracy.

4. *The Religious Society of Friends is rooted in Christianity and has always found inspiration in the life and teachings of Jesus. How do you interpret your faith in light of this heritage? How does Jesus speak to you today? Are you following Jesus' example of love in action? Are you learning from his life the reality and cost of obedience to God? How does his relationship with God challenge and inspire you?*

✳ ✳ ✳

From early Friends we have inherited a vivid record of engagement with the Word, the text and the world. Many of their experiences release us from earlier limiting interpretations of the biblical text. This is frequently clothed in an apocalyptic thought pattern that is foreign to many of today's Friends.

The powerful spiritual experiences of early Friends were described by them as the rediscovery of primitive Christianity. This experience was not only that of the historical Jesus, or of a cosmic Christ, but of a personal, immanent God. In 1657 George Fox wrote: 'We must not have Christ Jesus, the Lord of Life, put any more in the stable among the horses and asses, but he must now have the best chamber, the heart.'[6]

Friends today may have few things in common, but within the constraints of language, agree on the immediacy of God,[7] which can be personal or shared through group worship. Martin Buber described this immediacy as the

'I-Thou' relationship.

Thomas Kelly experienced God through the created world, and his sense of cosmic immediacy shatters anthropocentrism, '... the experience of an inflooding, all-enfolding Love, which is at the center of Divine Presence, is of a love which *embraces all creation*, not just our little petty selves... Not only does all creation have a new smell, as Fox found, but it has a new value as enwrapped in the infinite Love of God, wherein not a sparrow falls to the ground without the Father. This is not just Jesus' experience. Nor is it his *inference about God's* tender love; it is *the record of his experience in God.* There is a tendering of the soul, toward *everything* in creation, from the sparrow's fall to the slave under the lash.'[8]

Other Friends know God through their experience of and engagement in all aspects of life, worship, relationships and service.[9] There are also times when God is experienced as Creator, when the numinous[10] overwhelms the intimacy of a meeting for worship.

5. *Take time to learn about other people's experiences of the Light. Remember the importance of the Bible, the writings of Friends and all writings which reveal the ways of God. As you learn from others, can you in turn give freely from what you have gained? While respecting the experiences and opinions of others, do not be afraid to say what you have found and what you value. Appreciate that doubt and questioning can also lead to spiritual growth and to a greater awareness of the Light that is in us all.*

How can our differing perceptions of God be reconciled? Some modern scholars have challenged the orthodox Christian dichotomy of an immanent yet transcendent God by emphasising that the universe is in God, although God is more than the universe.[11] This pictures God as being both/and instead of either/or, as becoming not just being, as both potential and actual, having change and permanence and being relative and absolute.[12]

The dialectic of both/and may be illustrated by the analogy that God is to the world as the mind is to the body, with the world as God's body.[13] This has been expressed as, 'When I say "world", I mean the whole world - the cosmos as we know it, the stars and planets, biological life, human consciousness, culture and history. The whole world is the figure, shape or gestalt of God in the moment of *difference*; it is "God's body"'.[14] The model of the universe as God's body adds an positive element missing in the creation accounts of Genesis. That is, we experience life through our bodies. The body was the means of the distortion of relationships in Genesis 3 and we have still lost sight of the affirmation that the body is good. If the world is viewed as God's body, we as embodied creatures are affirmed, as is our positive response to the rest of creation.

Pantheism, the belief that God and the universe are identical, is not being described here. God is not identical with the universe, for the universe is dependent on God in a way that God is not dependent on the universe. What is being described is pan*en*theism and there are elements of this in the biblical record. The Bible is filled with passages that suggest a deep sensitivity to the power and beauty of the created world,[15] and it affirms this created beauty, recognising the numinous, the divine presence, in nature. This feeling is not ascribed pantheistically to nature itself, but to God. Nature, like human beings, is created by God. Panentheism does not deify nature. Paul described God as being 'above all and through all and in all'.[16]

The choice of the final compilers of Genesis to leave two such divergent accounts of creation may indicate that there was a recognition that both were incomplete, and that by presenting them one after the other, the reader could juxtapose them into a new whole. Martin Buber expressed this as 'In the beginning is the relation'.[17] Relational panentheism sees the world as having some creative independence from God, recognising that the history of the universe is not representative of the desire of God. What sort of interaction do we have with God?

8. *Worship is our response to an awareness of God. We can worship alone, but when we join with others in expectant waiting we may discover a deeper sense of God's presence. We seek a gathered stillness in our meetings for worship so that all may feel the power of God's love drawing us together and leading us.*

Separation between Creator and creation is unknown in the First Nations' traditions of North America. Although different nations have very different creation stories, all stress unity between God and creation: 'We believe that when the Mystery, or God, created the universe, he placed his hand on the whole thing, so everything is spiritual. As far as I know, God never told us Mohawks to separate anything, but just to look upon everything that he made as holy and sacred and act accordingly with respect.'[18]

6. *Do you work gladly with other religious groups in the pursuit of common goals? While remaining faithful to Quaker insights, try to enter imaginatively into the life and witness of other communities of faith, building together the bonds of friendship.*

❄ ❄ ❄

We employ metaphors in all our attempts to name God. Many traditional metaphors for God are hierarchical, imperialistic and dualistic and they offer us no sense of mutuality, shared responsibility or reciprocity.

Early Friends challenged the accepted range of metaphors as they enthusiastically witnessed to their experiences. These include the 'Seed', the 'Word', the 'Inner Light', the 'Living Way', the 'Eternal Being', the 'Green Tree', expressions that may not seem heretical to modern Friends, but which caused shock and distress in the seventeenth century. Today, as we seek to find the words which best express our experiences of God, the use of 'G-d', 'Goddess' or 'Gaia' may cause some Friends' distress.

Quakers took the name 'Friends', using the choice of Jesus in naming a relationship with others:

> You are my friends if you do what I command you. I do not call you servants any longer, because the servant does not know what the master is doing; but I have called you friends, because I have made known to you everything that I have heard from my Father... I am giving you these commands so that you may love one another.
>
> *John 15:14-15,17*

The logical extension of this relationship is to see God as a friend.

The Greek word for 'friend' is *phileo*. Although it is one of a cluster of words that describe different aspects of love, friendship has taken a back seat as a spiritual relationship. Paul took another word, *agape*, and gave a rich new meaning to what had been a little-used term. His listing of the qualities of *agape* in 1 Corinthians 13, may be the highest tribute paid to love in Christian literature.

In light of this emphasis, C. S. Lewis has little positive to say about love expressed in terms of friendship, '... it is something quite marginal... unnecessary, like philosophy, like art.'[19] Because of its devaluation, friendship is often perceived as a casual relationship.

In true friendship one opens oneself to a level of intimacy with another person. Intimate friends can be uncomfortable together. Intimate friends can go beyond being honest with each other to a level of honest dishonesty, playing their games of self-deception, while all the time, they know games are being played; and being willing to let them be so the other can work through defensiveness, which devises the game for protection. Intimate friends suffer with each other's suffering, hearing the laughter in the tears and the tears in the laughter.[20]

21. *Do you cherish your friendships, so that they grow in depth and understanding and mutual respect? In close relationships we may risk pain as well as finding joy. When experiencing great happiness or great hurt we may be more open to the working of the Spirit.*

While the relationship between lovers is one in which the focus is on the other, friends care about the same truth and so energy is released beyond the relationship. When lovers are also friends a powerful relationship is experienced. Friendship can go beyond a species relationship, as demonstrated between people and animals, and in the intimate link some human beings have with a particular place or with the Earth as a whole.

As Friends do we not need to look more seriously at our name and its implications for our relationships with each other, with God and with creation?

We all recognise that we need to have others with whom to walk as we struggle to balance autonomy and intimacy, aloneness and closeness, and in accepting the least admirable parts of ourselves. Modern research has shown that for men such intimacy with another person is only achieved after a sense of identity is reached, while for women an ethic of care for and relationship with others is central to their development.[21]

For much of the Church, the sacramental meal is a primary symbol of the restored relationship between human beings and God. In the Emmaus story Jesus transforms his role from one of stranger to one of host as he breaks bread.[22] Other meals in which Jesus shared with his friends took on the quality of Jubilee. The Quaker focus on an unmediated relationship with God precludes a formal physical reminder of the Last Supper, but the sight of Friends at pot luck gatherings or picnics is a confirmation that food and fellowship are basic elements of community. At such meals strangers are welcome.

18. *How can we make the meeting a community in which each person is accepted and nurtured, and strangers are welcome? Seek to know one another in the things which are eternal, bear the burden of each other's failings and pray for one another. As we enter with tender sympathy into the joys and sorrows of each other's lives, ready to give help and to receive it, our meeting may be a channel for God's love and forgiveness.*

The world as God's body. God as a Friend. A Friend whose relationship with us includes all creation. A Friend who deeply cares for us but who cannot be manipulated by us. A Friend whose love for us is invitational.

1. *Take heed, dear Friends, to the promptings of love and truth in your hearts. Trust them as leadings of God whose Light shows us our darkness and brings us to new life.*

❄ ❄ ❄

In the anxiety experienced as the medieval worldview collapsed, previously accepted absolutes were seen as no longer having worth. From a unified worldview based on the creation stories, individuals were challenged by the scientific accounts that described the Earth as no longer being the centre of creation. For Calvin, nature was totally depraved. The Scientific Revolution initially saw nature as a symbol of divine reason manifest in natural law, but later the dualism of transcendent intellect and dead matter became the dominant mode of thought. Nature which had been seen as being alive was reduced to a dead machine, valuable only as raw material to be used for meeting human needs. The self became the absolute point of reference as pure reason was pursued.

The clock was a high point of technology in Newton's era, and this provided the basic model for a universe run on clockwork principles. The steam engine gave shape to later thermodynamic models. The Industrial Revolution left us with a series of ethical challenges: the despoiling of the environment, the loss of rural community, alienation from work and the loss of individual dignity. The development of the Darwinian science of evolution shattered the idea of the special creation of human beings. Today the computer reigns and so the mechanical universe again finds a metaphor to explain its mysteries. In a mechanical model one must understand each part, and be able to take it apart and reconstruct it. It is not easy to put life back together.

The dominant world view of the twentieth century sees people as being different from creation over which they have dominion. Progress, especially with the aid of technology, will solve all problems. Science is projected as a universal, value-free system of knowledge. This view is challenged by some feminists who claim that a military agenda drives science and technology.[23]

38.   *If pressure is brought upon you to lower your standard of integrity, are you prepared to resist it? Our responsibilities to God and our neighbour may involve us in taking unpopular stands. Do not let the desire to be sociable, or the fear of seeming peculiar, determine your decisions.*

Elements of this dominant worldview should cause us deep concern. In seeking to create life, the rate of change of our technological expertise may be outrunning our compassionate understanding and our ability to establish appropriate ethical principles. For example, reproductive technology and genetic engineering are based on the same principles as other sciences. But life cannot be measured in test tubes. Should we patent new life forms? Are we not confusing production and property with the creative ability to regenerate life? Having colonised the planet are we now seeking to colonise life? God risked playing with clay to make the groundling: are we ready for this responsibility?

39. *Consider which of the ways to happiness offered by society are truly fulfilling and which are potentially corrupting and destructive ...*

At the beginning of the twentieth century, two new scientific theories shattered the certainty of the Newtonian universe. These are the general theories of relativity and quantum mechanics. Relativity deals with space and time and how they are curved on a large scale. Quantum mechanics deals with subatomic particles and recognises that there is always an element of chance which affects the behaviour of matter on a small scale. In grasping the implications of these new theories it was realised that not just new answers were needed, but also new questions. This questioning led to shifts in concepts of space, time, matter, and the links between subject and object and cause and effect.

Quantum theory recognises that there is no objective reality 'out there'. At the sub atomic level, particles come into being and are observed only in relation to something else. Relationship is a key determinant of what is observed and how particles manifest themselves. Our brains are sufficiently sensitive to respond to the absorption of a single photon, and so may be affected by quantum level behaviour.

In biology, the work of James Lovelock reflects this sense of relationship between what may seem to be separate parts of a whole. The Gaia theory projects a radically different model of Earth in which the Earth functions as a single organism that defines and maintains conditions necessary for its survival.[24] The approach of Barbara McClintock to her research with plant genetics is a further example of this changing attitude, as illustrated in the title of her autobiography, *A Feeling for the Organism*.

In chemistry, Ilya Prigogine won the Nobel Prize for his work on dissipative structures that regenerate to higher levels of self-organization in response to environmental demands. The response to disorder is not the expected collapse of the Newtonian model, but new forms of order.[25] These new forms of order are often spiral, resembling natural forms, intuitions of the wholeness within creation.

The illusion that the scientist is fully objective is now breaking down. John Muir (1838-1914) lay down on a sheet of polished granite to 'think like a glacier', and developed his glacial theory of the formation of the Sierra Nevada. 'When I discovered a new plant, I sat down beside it for a minute or a day, to make its acquaintance and to try to hear what it had to say... I asked the boulders I met whence they came and whither they were going. I followed to their fountains the various soils upon which the forests and meadows are planted; and when I discovered a mountain or a rock of marked form and structure, I climbed about it, comparing it with its neighbours, marking its relation to the forces that had acted upon it ...'[26]

Over ninety-nine percent of the atom is space. In the Newtonian universe the vast areas of outer space created a sense of loneliness. In the quantum world space is filled with fields whose effects can be observed. Just as fish are unaware of the water that surrounds them, we are unaware of the fields that are within and beyond us.

Modern science accepts the mysteries and does not seek to explain them away. There is delight is seeing the caterpillar and butterfly as two forms of stabilized structure within the evolution of one system, rather than dead samples crucified in a dusty museum. We do not know how long the coast of Britain is, recognising that there is no final answer.[27] Children's riddles are part of the reality of modern scientists, 'How do you hold a hundred tons of water in the air?' 'In a cloud.'

Scientists are beginning to see that the universe is not a great machine, but that it is a participant universe in which human beings may evoke a potential into reality. Just as the groundling was created to till the garden, we too have an ongoing role, but now we have eaten from the tree we are much more aware of the power of knowledge of good and evil. Like theologians, scientists build explanatory structures, telling stories that are scrupulously tested to see if they are stories about real life. At their best these stories incorporate the non-human voices of our planetary community when we are open to including them:

> ... ask the animals, and they will teach you;
> the birds of the air and they will tell you;
> ask the plants of the earth and they will teach you;
> and the fish of the sea will declare to you.
>
> *Job 12:7*

An exciting collaboration across disciplinary boundaries is that occurring between scientists and theologians. The recognition that humankind's domination over the planet is endangering all of creation on Earth has challenged us to seek out and hear the full story of the universe. Pierre Teilhard de Chardin[28] straddled the divide, but today his theories seem frighteningly anthropocentric. Fortunately others have continued his work; 'This journey is no longer simply the journey of the Christian Community through history to the heavenly Jerusalem. It is the journey of primordial matter through its marvellous sequence of transformation, in the stars, in the Earth, in the human, toward an ever more complete spiritual, physical intercommunication of the parts with each other, with the whole, and with the numinous presence which has ever been manifested throughout this cosmic-Earth-human process.'[29] This creation story 'radicalises both oneness and difference... it helps us develop a new eye for difference, for it tells us about diversity in proportions and in detail unlike anything we have known before... And yet, everything that is, from the fungi and protozoa on our planet to the black holes and exploding supernovas in distant galaxies, has a common origin: everything that is comes from one infinitesimal bit of matter. It staggers the imagination; it will also help us to think about unity and diversity in a new way.'[30]

7. *Be aware of the spirit of God at work in the ordinary activities and experience of your daily life. Spiritual learning continues throughout life, and often in unexpected ways. There is inspiration to be found all around us, in the natural world, in the sciences and arts, in our work and friendships, in our sorrows as well as in our joys. Are you open to new light, from whatever source it may come? Do you approach new ideas with discernment?*

The story being sought is not a new one, but the story that the universe itself is telling, in the voices of stars, fossils, mountain ranges, lakes and slugs. Mystics have already opened this story for us: Jesus with the kingdom of God within us, Julian with her hazelnut and William Blake with his grain of sand.[31] Blake illustrates how we can hold the both/and in creative tension:

> For double the vision my eyes do see,
> And a double vision is always with me:
> With my inward eye 'tis an old man grey;
> With my outward a thistle across my way.[32]

The new world-view also seeks to hold the inner and outer aspects of reality as one, with dualisms transformed into interdependencies.

We hear the insights of native peoples: among the Iroquois in North America where any decision is considered in terms of its effect on the seventh generation,[33] and in Australia where all objects share the same soul or spirit.[34]

The writers of Genesis had their own agendas, writing to meet the needs of their times. We can incorporate the biblical creation stories into the larger creation story as we recognise the need for a broader perspective that includes all who wish to hear it.

About fifteen thousand million years ago the universe 'flared forth into being'[35] with a big bang, exploding matter outward to create some hundred thousand million galaxies. From this beginning came all creation, so that all things living and non-living are related and share the common story. Living matter emerged only after thousands of millions of years, with humankind appearing only a few seconds before midnight in a clock of the universe.[36]

At the beginning of the agricultural revolution, about 12,000 years ago, the human population of the Earth was about 5 million. By the beginning of the scientific revolution it had increased to 500 million. Two hundred years later it doubled to one thousand million and by the year 2000 it is expected to have reached six thousand million. As latecomers we seem to be unaware of the increasing rate at which we are challenging all the relationships within the planet.

41.   *Try to live simply. A simple lifestyle freely chosen is a source of strength. Do not be persuaded into buying what you do not need or cannot afford. Do you keep yourself informed about the effects your style of living is having on the global economy and environment?*

In this creation story human beings have a special role. We are not the centre of creation, but we may be the only ones along with God who know this story. Our response to the story needs to be both aesthetic and ethical. We need to respond in wonder while we recognise our responsibility in enabling creation to continue. God destroyed creation in Noah's day. We are now in the position to destroy the Earth. This capacity for destruction must be balanced with the will to be co-creators. The accumulating crises we face of population, food, energy, pollution, extinction of species and war are all interconnected: they are our late twentieth century horsemen of the apocalypse.[37]

42.   *We do not own the world, and its riches are not ours to dispose of at will. Show a loving consideration for all creatures, and seek to maintain the beauty and variety of the world. Work to ensure that our increasing power over nature is used responsibly, with reverence for life. Rejoice in the splendour of God's continuing creation.*

In celebrating the universe story we must let go of the idea of human domination, with its underlying acceptance of dualism. Some people look back to a 'golden era' of 9000 to

4000 BCE when there is little evidence of war and when many societies were egalitarian. In many of these societies women seem to have had more central roles than in later, violent and patriarchal groups.[38] With the shift towards more rigidly hierarchical, authoritarian and patriarchal systems the gods took on characteristics of domination.

In a culture based on domination, the either/or scenario becomes the norm. Coexistence and complementarity are unknown. Difference implies superiority and therefore inferiority is created. Power becomes power over.

In a culture that is free from domination, values are radically different. We have a model of such a system in the ideal of *shalom* which is given form in the ministry and life of Jesus of Nazareth. The Sermon on the Mount is a manifesto of such a society.[39]

The language we use reflects the culture in which we live. The challenge to find appropriate words for expressing our experiences of God reflects that a limited expression has been the norm. The use of sexual and violent metaphors mirrors the values of our society.

Before the Reformation, the image of the Earth seen by all of western society was that of a living organism, conceptualised as female. The nurturing mother earth provided for all needs, but was also recognised as having wild and uncontrollable aspects. Francis Bacon, chancellor of England under James I, is seen as a pioneer of the scientific method. His language was filled with images drawn from witch-hunting and the Inquisition. He used violent sexual imagery to portray nature that is penetrated, conquered and forced to yield.[40] James Lovelock has maintained the sexual distinction in his descriptions of Gaia: 'The evolution of homo sapiens, with his technological inventiveness and his increasingly subtle communications network, has vastly increased

Gaia's range of perception, she is now through us awake and aware of herself. She has seen the reflection of her fair face ... '[41] In responding to questions about the place of religion in the Gaia hypothesis, Lovelock replied, 'The concept of Jahweh as all-powerful, all-seeing is either frightening or unapproachable... Mary is close and can be talked to. She is believable and manageable ... What if Mary is another name for Gaia?... For me Gaia is a religious as well as scientific concept, and in both spheres it is manageable.'[42] This projection of a subdued, desexualised and subservient model does not help us on our journey.

The military-nuclear subculture uses sexist language. The device dropped on the Bikini Islands was named 'Gilda' and painted with an image of Rita Hayworth, Marshall McLuhan's 'mechanical bride'. Expressions such as vertical erection launchers, soft lay downs, deep penetration, penetration aids, advantages of protracted rather than spasm attacks and releasing megatonnage in one orgasmic whump,[43] all perpetuate impaired patriarchal thinking. Equally distressing is the use of religious metaphor in the military-nuclear vocabulary. The first atomic explosion was named Trinity: 'One felt as though he had been privileged to witness the Birth of the World - to be present at the moment of Creation when the Lord said: "Let there be Light." '[44] We can, and must, do better.

A military metaphor is used in working with creation: 'This nation has a large and powerful adversary. Our opponent could cause the United States to lose nearly all her seaborne commerce, to lose her standing as first among trading nations ... We are fighting Mother Nature... It's a battle we have to fight day by day, year by year; the health of our economy depends on victory.'[45] This is the narrative from a film made by the Army Corps of Engineers on their attempt to control the Mississippi.

32. *Bring into God's light those emotions, attitudes and prejudices in yourself which lie at the root of destructive conflict, acknowledging your need for forgiveness and grace. In what way are you involved in the work of reconciliation between individuals, groups and nations?*

In his ministry and death, Jesus revealed a nonviolent God. Friends believe that any person who tries to live out gospel values is necessarily nonviolent. When we recognise that of God in all of creation we cannot kill. Brian Willson, an activist against the use of U.S. armaments for inhuman Central American regimes, said, 'I think nonviolence is not so much a tactic as a way of experiencing the world within yourself, of understanding the sacred connection with all of life. It's an understanding of how everything is interconnected... We are going against our own nature when we start disrespecting all the other parts of life: people, plants, animals, water, sunlight, clouds ...'[46]

33. *Are you alert to practices here and throughout the world which discriminate against people on the basis of who or what they are or because of their beliefs? Bear witness to the humanity of all people, including those who break society's conventions or its laws. Try to discern new growing points in social and economic life. Seek to understand the causes of injustice, social unrest and fear. Are you working to bring about a just and compassionate society which allows everyone to develop their capacities and fosters the desire to serve?*

'Love your enemies.'[47] If we truly believe in that of God in everyone and love them, there is no longer a depersonalised enemy. The dominant political, social and economic systems of the twentieth century have been based on an enemy mentality. Ronald Reagan's 'Evil Empire' has collapsed. Who will be the new enemy? The creation story of Genesis 1 emphasises that creation is good. Like the Babylonians, many people are still enslaved in a myth of violence that fears the outbreak of chaos. When we end the dualism of 'us' and 'them' we can all grow toward the Light.

31. *We are called to live 'in the virtue of that life and power that takes away the occasion of all wars'. Do you faithfully maintain our testimony that war and the preparation for war are inconsistent with the spirit of Christ? Search out whatever in your own way of life may contain the seeds of war. Stand firm in our testimony, even when others commit or prepare to commit acts of violence, yet always remember that they too are children of God.*

The need for community is universal. We were created for community and we each develop our personhood as social beings. Whenever community gathers there is a need for clear communication and for mediation of disputes that occur. Justice systems develop when a community seeks to codify acceptable and unacceptable behaviour. What is a just community? Looking for indications in the biblical record challenges us to glean for the pearls that are hidden there. 'Justice', *tsedaqah*, is not an abstract notion but an activity that is understood in relation to the covenant structure. There is a thread running through the Bible which shows that God is just, but biased. The bias is in favour of the weak, vulnerable and helpless.[48] Jesus extended this bias to include those who were morally and spiritually weak. A just community guarantees and maintains the rights of its weakest members, and as part of its social fabric seeks to support these members. A just community seeks to restore those who are accused of actions against the community. In a just community all members have a responsibility to others, there are no passive bystanders. In doing justice we become co-creators:

Is not this the fast I choose:
to loose the bonds of injustice,
to undo the thongs of the yoke,
to let the oppressed go free, and to break every yoke? ...
If you remove the yoke from among you,
the pointing of the finger, the speaking of evil,
if you offer your food to the hungry
and satisfy the needs of the afflicted,
then your light shall rise in the darkness
and your gloom be like the noonday.
The LORD will guide you continually,
and satisfy your needs in parched places,
and make your bones strong;
and you shall be like a watered garden,
like a spring of water,
whose waters never fail ...

Isaiah 58:6, 9-11

The prophets recognised that community extends beyond humankind; Micah envisions a law court in which the witnesses are the mountains and the foundations of the earth.[49] The challenge faced at this time on this planet is not simply a crisis for human beings but for the entire realm of animals and plants, the total biotic community interacting with nonliving forces. The Earth is one ecosystem, one creation. As we become more aware of the abiotic and biotic community of the Earth, a just community includes other species and the Earth's resources.

The vision of *shalom* is a vision of wholeness, encompassing the whole of creation. It is a vision of peace and well-being that will be realised only by relationships of justice and compassion. A viable historical future needs the *shalom* vision to become a historical reality, not a future dream.

The emotions of justice are love and forgiveness. How different from the criminal justice systems of the world.

34.   Remember your responsibilities as a citizen for the conduct of local, national and international affairs. Do not shrink from the time and effort your involvement may demand.

35.   Respect the laws of the state but let your first loyalty be to God's purposes. If you feel impelled by strong conviction to break the law, search your conscience deeply. Ask your meeting for the prayerful support which will give you strength as a right way becomes clear.

❋   ❋   ❋

When a totem pole is carved in Haida Gwaii, the carving is done in public. As people continue their daily routines, they wander by and chat with the carvers. Speeches are made and stories are told when the totem pole is raised. The pole becomes a reminder of the old stories it depicts and of the life of the community during its creation.

There is a totem pole in the black canoe, the speaker's staff in Kilstlaai's hand. The Killer Whale at the top of the pole is supported by the Raven, a Sea Grizzly or Snag and another Raven in fledgling form. The conjunction of Raven and Snag reminds the Haida people of their creation story. Raven found the top of a stone pole in the sea and climbed down the pole under the water. The pole belonged to Raven's uncle, the Snag. Raven was given two small sticks and told to bite them apart and spit them out. This he did and they grew to become the mainland and Haida Gwaii.[50]

At one point in its creation, Bill Reid named his statue *Sunday Afternoon on Lost Lagoon*,[51] saying it was based on his memories of taking the family out for drives. As it has come together, *The Spirit of Haida Gwaii*, although relating to the family, indicates a deeper reality. Characters from the past are holding on to symbols of creation. There is a new character helping to propel the canoe. Male and female human beings and animals are in a state of dynamic balance, necessary so that the canoe does not tip. We are not sure where they are going. Or are they coming back?

The Exodus and the Exile were the historical experiences that forged the Israelites into a people. From their experiences of God they formulated their cosmology, a cosmology we have inherited. The journey out of Egypt was a risky departure into an unknown future. What Exodus or Exile experience will force us into the canoe? When we leave behind the enslaving culture that is destroying the Earth we will need to discern who will be our fellow-voyagers and what we will retain from our past and present if there is to be a future for creation.

22. *Respect the wide diversity among us in our lives and relationships. Refrain from making prejudiced judgements about the life journeys of others. Do you foster the spirit of understanding and forgiveness which our discipleship asks of us? Remember that each one of us is unique, precious, a child of God.*

Travelling blessings, dear Friends!

Appendix

Sources in Genesis

Traditionally, Moses was believed to have written the first five books of the Bible, also known as the *Torah* or *Pentateuch*. Modern scholars believe that there are indications of several writers in these books.

J, which uses *Yahweh* in naming God, was written about 960-930 BCE in Solomon's court, perhaps by a woman. It presents a Judaean national epic for the newly formed kingdom. The author enjoys puns, and is more interested in socio-cultural and political situations than in religious history. Old myths are retained and built into a robust narrative.

P was written during the late period of the exile in Babylon or in the early restoration, 550-450 BCE. A priestly emphasis is added to earlier documents with a well-ordered account of creation, ritual for the Sabbath, circumcision, priesthood and sacrifices. There are many genealogies.

Some scholars identify several more sources in these chapters. These include a writer of the so-called *Book of Generations*, who unified the stories by linking them together using genealogical information.

Source critics identify four main literary sources in the Pentateuch. In addition to **J** and **P**, are **E**, which uses *Elohim* in naming God, and **D**, which is mainly material in Deuteronomy.

The classic work on this topic is Martin Noth's *A History of Pentateuchal Traditions*, Prentice-Hall, Englewood Cliffs, 1972. A more accessible account is that of Richard Elliott Friedman, in *Who Wrote the Bible?*, Summit, New York, 1987.

A simplified breakdown of the main sources of documents in Genesis 1-11 follows.

J	P	Book of Generations
	1: 1-31	
	2: 1-4a	2:4a
3:1-24	2:4b-25	
4:1-26		
	5:1-28	
5:29	5:30-32	
6:1-8	6:9-22	6:6
7:1-5	7:6	
7:7	7:8-9	
7:10	7:11	
7:12	7:13-16a	
7:16b	7:17a	
7:17b	7:18-21	
7:22-23	7:24	
	8:1-2a	
8:2b-3a	8:3b-5	
8:6-12	8:13a	
8:13b	8:14-19	
8:20-22		
	9:1-17	
9:18-27	9:28-29	9:28-9
	10:1a	10:1a
10:1b	10:2-7	
10:8-19	10:20	
10:21	10:22-23	
10:24-30	10:31-32	
1:1-9	11:10-26	11:10-26

REFERENCES

Chapter I: THE SPIRIT OF HAIDA GWAII

1. Haida Gwaii, the Islands of the People, is the Haida name for the Queen Charlotte Islands. *The Spirit of Haida Gwaii*, made from 5,000 kg (11,000 lb) of cast bronze with black patina, is 6m (20 ft) long and almost 4m (13ft) high. It was installed in 1991 having taken five years to create.

2. Walter Fisher, *Human Communication as Narration: towards a philosophy of reason, value and action*, University of South Carolina, 1987, page 18 and Stanley Hauerwas, *A Community of Character: toward a constructive Christian social ethic*, University of Notre Dame, 1981, page 152.

3. Janet Scott, *What Canst Thou Say? towards a Quaker theology*, Quaker Home Service, 1980, pages 11-14.

4. Henry Cadbury, *A Quaker Approach to the Bible*, The Ward Lecture 1983, Philadelphia Yearly Meeting; T Canby Jones, 'The Bible: its authority and dynamic in George Fox and contemporary Quakerism', *Quaker Religious Thought*, IV, I (Spring 1962); Martha Paxson Grundy, 'How Early Friends Understood the Bible', in *Reclaiming a Resource: papers from the Friends Bible Conference*, Chuck Fager, ed., Kimo, 1990.

5. 1 Kings 17:10-24, 2 Kings 5:1-14.

6. Luke 4:18-19, 25-27.

7. George Fox, *The Works of George Fox*, New Foundation edition of the 1831 edition, 1990, volume 5, page 74.

8. Margaret Fell, *A Sincere and Constant Love: an introduction to the work of Margaret Fell*, Terry S. Wallace, Friends United Press, 1992, page 22.

9. Canadian Yearly Meeting 1981, minute #93, *Canadian Yearly Meeting Minutes 1981*, page 79.

10. This circle has been called the hermeneutics of suspicion by liberation theologians.

11. Alaisdair MacIntyre, *After Virtue*, University of Notre Dame Press, 1981.

12. *Science*, 155, 10 March 1967, pages 1203-1207.

13. Most liberal scholars accept that there are several traditions interwoven in Genesis. These include J and P, the main sources in Genesis 1-11. A listing of the sources is found in the appendix, pages 121-2.

14. It has been suggested that J, one of the strands of tradition incorporated into the first five books of the Bible, was written by a woman: *The Book of J*. David Rosenberg and Harold Bloom, Grove Weidenfeld, 1990.

15. '... because the scriptures are only a declaration of the source, and not the source itself, they are not to be considered the principal foundation of truth and knowledge. They are not even to be considered the principal foundation of all truth and knowledge.' Robert Barclay, Proposition 3 - The Scriptures, in *Barclay's Apology in Modern English*, Dean Freiday, ed., 1967, page 46.

16. *The Works of George Fox*, volume 3, page 462

17. Introduction, *Advices and Queries*, The Yearly Meeting of the Religious Society of Friends (Quakers) in Britain, 1994, pages 3-4.

18. *Bringing the Invisible into the Light*, Swarthmore Lecture 1986, page 4, and Pam Lunn, 'Love and Politics', *Friends Quarterly*, vol 26 (1990-91), page 51.

19. Northrop Frye, *The Great Code: the Bible and literature*, Harcourt Brace Jovanovich, 1983, page 17.

20. *Global Awareness: Quotations*, Our Planet in Every Classroom, World Federalists of Canada, note 2.

21. *ibid.*, quotations from the Bruntland Commission and Russell Schweickart.

22. Lewis Thomas, *The Lives of a Cell*, Bantam, 1980, page 170.

23. Timothy Findley offers a creative re-visioning of the Noah family's experience, in *Not Wanted on the Voyage*, Penguin, 1984.

24. *Advices & Queries*, numbers 16 and 17, page 9.

Chapter II: IN THE BEGINNING: GENESIS 1

1. For nearly fifteen centuries the Church accepted that Moses wrote the first five books of the Bible, the Torah, under God's command and inspiration. In 1753, Jean Astruc asked questions about the documents Moses used in writing the book of Genesis. By the middle of the nineteenth century most scholars accepted a four document theory of editorship. Julius Wellhausen went further, dating the documents well after the time of Moses.

2. BCE (Before the Common Era) is used rather than BC (Before Christ) with CE (Common Era) instead of AD (*Anno Domini*).

3. Prior to the Exile people are referred to as 'Hebrews' or 'Israelites' and after the return as 'Jews'.

4. Hosea emphasises that Yahweh, not Baal, brings fertility to the land, Hosea 2:8; and ironically declares that Israel incurred guilt through Baal, 13:1. Other allusions include Baal's conflict with Leviathan, Psalm 74:12-17, Baal's conflict over the waters in Psalm 93:12, and Baal as storm god in Psalm 29.

5. Samuel Noah Kramer, *The Sumerians: their history, culture and character*, University of Chicago, 1963.

6. David Rosenburg and Harold Bloom, *The Book of J*, Grove Weidenfeld, 1990, page 30. Robert Graves and Raphael Patai, *Hebrew Myths: the Book of Genesis*, Cassell and Co, 1964, pages 28-33, have similar accounts.

7. James B. Pritchard, *Ancient Near East Texts relating to the Old Testament*, 3rd. edition, Priceton University, 1969, pages 60-72; and John Romer, *Testament: the Bible and history*, Henry Holt, 1988, pages 35-39.

8. Joseph Campbell, *The Masks of God: Occidental Mythology*, Penguin, 1976, page 80.

9. The *Myth of the Goddess: evolution of an image*, by Anne Baring and Jules Cashford, Arkana, Penguin, 1993, examines representations of goddesses from the Palaeolithic era in 20,000 BCE to modern times.

10. YAHWEH is one of the names of God used in the Hebrew text. In English versions it is often translated as 'the LORD'. There is uncertainty about the origin of the name, though Exodus 3:14 interprets it as 'I AM WHO I AM', or some variation of the verb 'to be'. The name came to denote the distinctive concept of God for the Israelites.

11. Robert Alter, *The Art of Biblical Narrative*, Basic Books, 1981, pages 23-46.

12. At the end of *A Brief History of Time*, Bantam, 1988, page 175, Stephen Hawking, speaking of the events of the first micro-seconds of creation, says that if we were to discover these events 'then we would know the mind of God'.

13. Brian Swimme and Thomas Berry, *The Universe Story: from the primordial flaring forth to the Ecozoic era - a celebration of the unfolding of the cosmos*, Harper San Francisco, 1992.

14. Claus Westermann, *Genesis 1-11: a commentary*, Augsburg, 1984, pages 97-108.

15. Quoted in Northrop Frye, *The Double Vision: language and meaning in religion*, University of Toronto Press, 1991, page 71.

16. George Fox, *Journal*, Norman Penney ed., Friends Tract Association, 1891, volume 1, page 423.

17. A type of religious thought marked by a struggle between God and evil leading to a final cosmic battle when the evil powers are vanquished.

18. Christopher Hill, *Puritanism and Revolution*, Schocken, 1958, page 29.

19. *The Journal of George Fox*, John L Nickalls ed., Religious Society of Friends, 1975, pages 48, 74, etc.

20. George Fox, *The Power of the Lord is Over All: the pastoral letters of George Fox*, Canby Jones ed., Friends United Press, 1989, page 197.

21. *Journal*, Nickalls, page 8.

22. George Fox, *Journal*, Bicentenary Edition, Norman Penney ed., Friends Tract Association, 1891, vol 1, pages 274-5.

23. Karl Barth, *Letters 1961-1968*, Geoffrey W Bromiley trans., Eerdmans, 1981, page 184.

24. *Quaker Faith and Practice in the Experience of the Society of Friends*, Britain Yearly Meeting, 1995, §20.51.

25. *The Power of the Lord is Over All*, page 288.

26. A.R. Millard, P. Bordeuil, 'A Statue from Syria with Assyrian and Aramaic Inscriptions', *Biblical Archæologist*, 45, 1982, pages 135-141.

27. 'Abraham Joseph Heschel's last words: an interview by Carl Stern', *Intellectual Digest*, June 1973, page 78.

28. *The Works of George Fox*, volume 7, page 325.

29. Quoted in *The Ottawa Citizen*, August 3rd., 1994, page C-1

30. Rachel Carson, *Silent Spring*, Houghton Mifflin, 1962, frontispiece.

31. Gerald Wilson, 'Restoring the Image: perspectives on a biblical view of creation', *Quaker Religious Thought*, 24:4, 1990, pages 17-18.

32. *The Words of George Fox*, volume 7, page 78.

33. *The Works of George Fox*, volume 6, page 4.

34. *Journal*, Nickalls, page 2.

35. *The Works of George Fox*, volume 5, page 4.

36. Rosemary Radford Ruether, *God and Gaia: an ecofeminist theology of earth healing*, Harper San Francisco, 1992, pages 50-154.

37. 1 Maccabees 2:29-38.

38. Donald E Gowan, *Bridge Between the Testaments: a reappraisal of Judaism from the Exile to the birth of Christianity*, Pickwick, 2nd. ed., 1980, pages 187-200.

39. William C Braithwaite, *The Beginnings of Quakerism*, Sessions, 2nd ed., 1981, pages 424-425.

40. Ursula Franklin, *The Real World of Technology: Massey lectures*, Canadian Broadcasting Corporation, 1990.

41. Thomas R. Kelly, *A Testament of Devotion*, Quaker Home Service, 1979 edition, pages 55-56.

42. Thomas Merton, *Conjectures of a Guilty Bystander*, Doubleday, 1966, page 73.

43. Paul Ricoeur, *The Symbolism of Evil*, Harper and Row, 1967, page 197.

44. Walter Wink, *Engaging the Powers: discernment and resistance in a world of domination*, Fortress, 1992, page 17.

45. Alice Walker, *The Color Purple*, Harcourt Brace Jovanovich, 1982, page 39.

Chapter III: IN THE GARDEN: GENESIS 2-3

1. Eleanor Ferris Beach, 'Meditation on the Flood', *The Lamb's War: Quaker essays in honour of Hugh Barbour*, ed. Michael L. Birkel and John W Newman, Earlham College, 1992, page 243.

2. *2 Esdras*, also known as *The Apocalypse of Ezra* or *4 Ezra*, is a Jewish book written at the end of the first century CE. It has not been preserved in rabbinic tradition, but is included in the Christian Apocrypha. The letter to the *Romans* was written by Paul around 55-57 CE.

3. Based on Walter Brueggemann, *Genesis*, John Knox, 1982, pages 41-2.

4. The interpretation of Genesis 2-3 which follows leans heavily on that of Phyllis Trible, *God and the Rhetoric of Sexuality*, Fortress, 1978.

5. David Rosenburg, *The Lost Book of Paradise: Adam and Eve in the garden of Eden*, Hyperion, 1993, pages xii-xiii.

6. Genesis 4: 17-26 indicates an interest in cultural achievements at the time of David and Solomon, Claus Westermann, *Genesis: an introduction*, Augsburg, 1992, page 96.

7. YAHWEH-ELOHIM is also found in Exodus 9:30.

8. K. Joines, *Serpent Symbolism in the Old Testament*, Haddenfield House, 1974, page 102.

9. This shift from tribal organisation to monarchy is complex and has been introduced briefly to give a background to the shift in the roles of the characters in the story. See Norman K. Gottwald, *The Hebrew Bible: a socio-literary introduction*, Fortress, 1985 for the complete context.

10. Hans Walter Wolff, *Anthropology of the Old Testament*, Fortress, 1974, pages 10-25.

11. Graves and Patai, page 67.

12. Pritchard, page 42-44.

13. Baring and Cashford, Arkana, 1993, page 495.

14. Baring and Cashford, page 496.

15. Rosenberg, pages 33-34, 59.

16. This may suggest that two stories have been combined, or that the author only mentions a particular element when it is needed to move the story forward.

17. S. H. Hooke, *Middle Eastern Mythology*, Pelican, 1963, page 115.

18. Douglas Gwyn, *Apocalypse of the Word: the life and message of George Fox*, Friends United Press, 1984, page 49.

19. *Journal*, Nickalls, page 511.

20. *The Power of the Lord Is Over All*, page 357, and *The Works of George Fox*, volume 8, page 69.

21. Edward Hicks, introduction by Eleanor Price Mather, *A Peaceable Season*, The Pyne Press, 1973, 'Peaceable Kingdom with Quakers Bearing Banners', unpaged.

22. Baring and Cashford, page 497.

23. Joines, page 47.

24. *The Works of George Fox*, volume 6, page 11.

25. *The Works of George Fox*, volume 6, page 5.

26. In Latin, *malum* means both 'bad' and 'apple'.

27. *A Sincere and Constant Love*, page 63-4.

28. Gwyn, page 98.

29. Hugh Barbour and Arthur O Roberts, *Early Quaker Writings: 1650-1700*, Eerdmans, 1973, page 503.

30. *The Works of George Fox*, volume 6, page 25.

31. *The Power of the Lord is Over All*, pages 434-5.

32. *The Works of George Fox*, volume 6, page 10.

33. *The Power of the Lord is Over All*, page xviii.

34. *The Works of George Fox*, volume 6, pages 2 and 12.

35. Erich Fromm, *The Art of Loving*, Allen and Unwin, 1962, page 43.

36. *Journal*, Nickalls, pages 666-667.

37. Heinrich Kramer and James Sprenger, *Malleus Malleficarum*, 1468, Dover 1971, page 44.

38. An even more unpleasant story is recorded in Judges 19. Although it is an old story, it incorporates later values. A concubine is gang-raped and murdered. Her master cuts the corpse into twelve pieces and sends them around the tribes for retribution. Will they kill the perpetrators, thus destroying one tribe? Read it. Weep. Jesus offered his broken body to the twelve disciples, but we have still not learned the lesson.

39. A.J. Williams, 'The Relationship of Genesis 3:20 to the Serpent', *Zeitschrift für die Alttestamentliche Wissenschaft*, 89, 3 (1977), pages 357-374.

40. Walter Brueggeman, 'David and His Theologian', *Catholic Biblical Quarterly*, 30, 1968, pages 156-181.

41. Christians experience the crucifixion of Jesus, on a 'tree', as giving them access to eternal life.

42. *Journal*, Nickalls, page 347.

43. *Journal*, Nickalls, page 27.

Chapter IV: MURDER AND MORE: GENESIS 4-11

1. 'Vanity of vanities says the teacher, vanity of vanities! All is vanity!' Ecclesiastes 1:2.

2. Samuel Noah Kramer, *History Begins at Sumer*, Doubleday, 1955, page 189.

3. Gerhard von Rad, *Old Testament Theology*, I, SCM, 1975, page 252.

4. 'There was only one place that bothered me. The King James Version says this - it is where Jehovah has asked Cain why he is angry. Jehovah says, "If thou doest well, shalt thou not be accepted? And if thou doest not well, sin lieth at the door. And unto thee shall be his desire, and thou shalt rule over him." It was the *thou shalt* that struck me, because it was a promise that Cain would conquer sin....Then I got a copy of the American Standard Bible. It was very new then. And it was different in this passage. It says "Do thou rule over him." Now this is very different. This is not a promise, it is an order. And I began to stew about it. I wondered what the original word of the original writer had been... These old men believe a true story, and they know a true story when they hear it. They are critics of truth. They know that these sixteen verses are a history of mankind in any age or culture or race. They do not believe that a man writes fifteen and three-quarter verses of truth and tells a lie with one verb...' John Steinbeck, *East of Eden*, Bantam, New York, 1976 (first published 1952), pages 301, 304.

5. *Journal*, Nickalls, page 30.

6. *The Works of George Fox*, volume 4, page 130.

7. *The Works of George Fox*, volume 6, page 451.

8. *The Power of the Lord is Over All*, page 559.

9. Madeleine L'Engle, *Ladder of Angels*, Penguin, 1980, page 20.

10. Bishop Ussher of Armagh was a Calvinist scholar and his challenger was the Jesuit theologian, Petavius. Romer, page 333.

11. Genesis 11:26.

12. Graves and Patai, page 113.

13. *The Power of the Lord is Over All*, page 145.

14. Kramer, *History*, pages 150-154.

15. Pritchard, pages 66-72.

16. Westermann, page 446.

17. Beach, page 251.

18. Beach, page 253.

19. George Mendenhall, *The Tenth Generation*, Johns Hopkins, 1973, pages 38-48.

20. Wink, pages 177-179.

21. Westermann, pages 538-539.

22. Romer, page 39.

23. Gwyn, page 78.

24. *Journal*, Nickalls, page 333.

25. *A Sincere and Constant Love*, page 16.

1. Extracts from Britain Yearly Meeting's *Advices & Queries* are inserted in the text in italics throughout this chapter.

2. *One World*, World Council of Churches, Geneva, January-February, 1988.

3. Micah 6:8.

4. Mark 1:10.

5. Mark 16:8, John 20:19.

6. *Journal*, Nickalls, page 312.

7. Douglas Steere suggests that these are immediacy, Jesus Christ, that of God, redeeming love and the waiting ministry/conduct of business, *Five Essentials of Quaker Faith Today*, unpublished, Haverford Quaker Collection.

8. Thomas Kelly, pages 97-98.

9. Janet Scott, pages 71-72; and 'Report of the work of the Book of Discipline Revision Committee', in *London Yearly Meeting of the Religious Society of Friends Proceedings 1994, Documents in Advance - 2*, page 12.

10. Rudolf Otto coined the term 'numinous' in *The Idea of the Holy*, Oxford University Press, 1923, (in German 1917). Numinous points to a unique feeling and quality of holiness, mystery and otherness associated with an object or person. Otto analyzed the feelings which accompany an experience of the numinous and described them by the phrase *mysterium tremendum et fascinans*. These are the sense of wholly other, dread and awe accompanied by a sense of being drawn to the object or person.

11. This understanding of God is named process theology. It has been examined with different emphases, for example by A.N. Whitehead from a science-based outlook and by Charles

Hartshorne from a philosophical perspective. Pierre Teilhard de Chardin blended both scientific and theological concerns.

12. Arthur R Peacocke, *Creation and the World of Science: the Brampton Lectures*, Clarendon Press, 1978; and Jay B. McDaniel, *Of God and Pelicans: a theology of the reverence for life*, Westminster/John Knox, 1989.

13. Grace Jantzen, *God's World, God's Body*, Westminster, 1984. Sallie McFague has developed the concept further in *Models of God: theology for an ecological, nuclear age*, Fortress, 1987 and *The Body of God: an ecological theology*, Fortress, 1993.

14. Peter Hodgson, *God in History: shapes of freedom*, Abingdon, 1989, page 106.

15. Job, Matthew 6:28.

16. Ephesians 4:6.

17. Martin Buber, *I and Thou*, ed. and trans. Walter Kaufman, Charles Scribner's Sons, 1970, page 69.

18. Sakokwenonkwas, 'The Road Back to Our Future', *Gamaliel* 3,1, Spring 1977, page 35.

19. C.S. Lewis, *The Four Loves*, Collins, 1963, pages 55 and 67.

20. Based on George Jeannot, quoted in L. Patrick Carroll and Katherine Marie Dykeman, *Chaos or Creation: spirituality in mid-life*, Paulist, 1986, pages 125-6.

21. Carol Gilligan, *In a Different Voice: psychological theory and women's development*, Harvard University Press, 1983; Lawrence Kohlberg, C Levine, A Hewer, *Moral Stages: a current formulation and a response to critics*, S Karger, 1983; Daniel Levinson, *The Season of a Man's Life*, Alfred A Knopf, 1975.

22. Luke 24:30.

23. Maria Mies and Vandana Shiva, *Ecofeminism*, Fernwood/Zed, 1993, page 94.

24. J E Lovelock, *Gaia: a new look at life on Earth*, Oxford University Press, 1979, *The Ages of Gaia: a biography of our living Earth*, W W Norton & Co, 1988.

25. Ilya Prigogine and Isabelle Stengers, *Order out of Chaos*, Bantam, 1984.

26. John Muir, *John of the Mountains*, ed Linnie Marsh Wolfe, University of Wisconsin Press, 1986, page 181.

27. Benoît Mandelbrot opened up the study of fractals, when he named a type of symmetrical, geometric structure which is part of natural forms. Any irregular boundary can be divided into more and more smaller parts, each of which have their own patterns. The length of a coastline becomes a study of the infinite.

28. Pierre Teilhard de Chardin, *The Phenomenon of Man*, William Collins & Sons, 1959.

29. Thomas Berry, quoted by John Yungblut in *Walking Gently on the Earth*, J Barnard Walton Memorial Lecture, Southeastern Yearly Meeting, 1990.

30. McFague, *Body*, pages 38-39.

31. Luke 17:21.

God showed me a little thing the size of a hazel nut lying in the palm of my hand, and it seemed to me to be as round as a ball. I looked at it and thought, 'What can this be?' and I was answered generally thus, 'It is all that is made.' I marvelled how it could last, because it seemed to me that it might fall to pieces because of its littleness. And I was answered in my understanding, 'It lasts and always will because God loves it. And in the same way, everything has its being through the love of God.' In this little thing I saw three parts: the first is

that God made it; the second is that God loves it; the third is
that God keeps it.

Julian of Norwich,
ed Pamela Searle, CIO Publishing, 1984.

> To see the World in a grain of sand,
> And Heaven in a wild flower,
> Hold Infinity in the palm of your hand,
> And Eternity in an hour.
>
> William Blake, *Auguries of Innocence.*

32. William Blake, poem incorporated in a letter to Thomas
Butts, 22nd November 1802.

33. Mike Myers, a Mohawk elder, shared this wisdom at the
1990 Annual General Meeting of the Church Council on
Justice and Corrections, a coalition of the Canadian churches.
In oral culture, stories of family are very important. A story-
teller can often name ancestors as far back as seven generations.
For the Mohawks, a return through seven generations takes
them to the period when they first met European immigrants.
Seven generations later, they understand the power of this
tradition as they mourn their loss of culture, land, identity
and self-respect.

34. Matthew Fox et al, *Creation Spirituality and
Dreamtime*, Millennium, 1991.

35. Brian Swimme and Thomas Berry, *The Universe Story:
from the primordial flashing forth to the ecozoic era - a celebration
of the unfolding of the cosmos*, HarperSanFrancisco, 1992.

36. The ritual Council of All Beings helps human beings re-
connect with their bio-ecological history, *Thinking like a
Mountain: towards a Council for All Beings*, John Seed, Joanna
Macy, Pat Fleming, Arne Naess, New Society, 1988. *Old
Turtle*, Douglas Wood and Cheng-Khee Chee, Pfeifer Hamilton
1992, helps all ages see and hear the universe story.

37. Revelation 6:2-8.

38. Elise Boulding, *The Underside of History*, Westview, 1976, page 40; Riane Eisler, *The Chalice and the Blade*, Harper and Row, 1987.

39. Matthew, chapters 5-7.

40. Francis Bacon, *Works*, ed. James Spedding, Longmans, 1887-1901, vol 4, page 247.

41. Lovelock, 1979, page 148.

42. Lovelock, 1988, page 206.

43. Carol Cohn, 'Sex and Death in the Rational World of Defence Intellectuals', in *Exposing Nuclear Phallacies*, ed. Diana E H Russell, Pergamon, 1989, pages 133-4.

44. William L. Laurence, 'Eyewitness Acccount of Bomb Test', *New York Times*, September 26th, 1945, page 1.

45. John McPhee, 'The Control of Nature', *The New Yorker*, February 23rd, 1987, page 40.

46. John Dear, 'The Road to Transformation: a conversation with Brian Willson', *Fellowship*, 56, March 1990, page 7.

47. Luke 6:35.

48. Psalm 72:1-4, 84:1-4, Isaiah 11:1-4.

49. Micah 6:1-2.

50. Based on the story by John Sky in Robert Bringhurst, *The Black Canoe: Bill Reid and the Spirit of Haida Gwaii*, Douglas & McIntyre, 1992, pages 64-65.

51. Bringhurst, page 86.

For Further Reading

Margaret Atwood
The Handmaid's Tale,
McLelland and Stewart, Toronto, 1985.

Thomas Berry
The Dream of the Earth,
Sierra Club Books, San Francisco, 1988.

Robert Bringhurst, Ulli Steltzer
The Black Canoe: Bill Reid and The Spirit of Haida Gwaii,
Douglas and McIntyre, Vancouver, 2nd edition, 1992.

Bill Devall, George Sessions
Deep Ecology: living as if nature mattered,
Gibbs M. Smith, Layton, 1985.

Timothy Findley
Not Wanted on the Voyage,
Penguin, Markham, 1984.

George Fox
The Journal of George Fox,
John L. Nickalls, ed., Religious Society of Friends, 1975.

Matthew Fox
The Coming of the Cosmic Christ: the healing of mother earth and the birth of a new renaissance,
Harper and Row, San Francisco, 1988.

Ursula Franklin
The Real World of Technology: the Massey Lectures,
Canadian Broadcasting Corporation, Toronto, 1990

Northrop Frye
The Great Code: the Bible and literature,
Harcourt Brace Jovanovich, New York, 1983.
Words with Power: being a second study of 'The Bible and literature',
Viking, Markham, 1990.

Albert Gore
Earth in the Balance: ecology and the human spirit,
Penguin, New York, 1992.

Ernst Haas
Creation, Penguin, New York, 1988.

Virginia Hamilton
In the Beginning: creation stories from around the world,
Harcourt Brace Jovanovich, San Diego, 1988.

Norman K. Gottwald
The Hebrew Bible: a socio-literary introduction,
Fortress, Philadelphia, 1985.

Douglas Gwyn
Apocalypse of the Word: the life and message of George Fox,
Friends United Press, Richmond, 1984.

Stephen Hawking
A Brief History of Time,
Bantam, New York, 1988.

Thomas R. Kelly
A Testament of Devotion,
Quaker Home Service, London, 1979 edition

Madeleine L'Engle
Ladder of Angels: scenes from the Bible illustrated by children of the world, Penguin, New York, 1980.

Sallie McFague
Models of God: theology for an ecological, nuclear age,
Fortress, Philadelphia, 1987.

Ilya Prigogine, Isabelle Stengers
Order Out of Chaos,
Bantam, New York, 1984.

David Rosenberg, ed.
Congregation: contemporary writers read the Jewish Bible
Harcourt Brace Jovanovich, San Diego, 1987.

Janet Scott
What Canst Thou Say? towards a Quaker theology,
Quaker Home Service, London, 1980.

John Seed, Joanna Macy, Pat Fleming, Arne Naess
Thinking like a Mountain: towards a Council of All Beings,
New Society Publishers, Philadelphia, 1988.

Brian Swimme, Thomas Berry
*The Universe Story: from the primordial flaring forth to the
Ecozoic era - a celebration of the unfolding of the cosmos,*
HarperSanFrancisco, 1992.

Douglas Wood, Cheng-Khee Chee
Old Turtle,
Pfeifer-Hamilton, Duluth, 1992.

Ronald Wright
Stolen Continents: the 'new world' though Indian eyes since 1492,
Viking, Toronto, 1991.